WHAT DO YOU KNOW?

THE ULTIMATE TEST OF COMMON (AND NOT SO COMMON) KNOWLEDGE

D0473931

WHAT DO YOU KNOW?

THE ULTIMATE TEST OF COMMON (AND NOT SO COMMON) KNOWLEDGE

JAIME O'NEILL
INTRODUCTION BY MIKE WALLACE

BANTAM BOOKS
NEW YORK · TORONTO · LONDON · SYDNEY · AUCKLAND

BANTAM BOOKS
NEW YORK · TORONTO · LONDON · SYDNEY · AUCKLAND

What Do You Know? The Ultimate Test of Common (And Not So
Common) Knowledge
A Bantam Book / June 1990

Chapter 5 photo numbers 1, 3, 12, 13, 14, and 19 courtesy
of the National Archives.
Chapter 5 photo numbers 2, 4, 5, 6, 7, 8, 9, 10, 11, 15, 16, 17, 18,
20, 21, 22, 23, 24, and 25 courtesy of the Library of Congress.

Book design by Jeannette Jacobs

Library of Congress Cataloging-in-Publication Data

O'Neill, Jaime.
    What do you know? : the ultimate test of common (and not so common)
knowledge / Jaime O'Neill : introduction by Mike Wallace.
      p. cm.
    ISBN 0-553-34880-9
    1. Educational tests and measurements. I. Title.
LB3051.053 1990
371.2'6—dc20   89–29350
                                                                                 CIP

Published simultaneously in the United States and Canada

Bantam Books are published by Bantam Books, a division of Bantam
Doubleday Dell Publishing Group, Inc. Its trademark, consisting of the
words "Bantam Books" and the portrayal of a rooster, is Registered in
U.S. Patent and Trademark Office and in other countries. Marca Regis-
trada. Bantam Books, 666 Fifth Avenue, New York, New York 10103.

PRINTED IN THE UNITED STATES OF AMERICA
RRH   0 9 8 7

For Karen

ACKNOWLEDGMENTS

Even a book as apparently simple as this one requires the work of countless hours and the support of a great many people. I am indebted to my wife, Karen, for her many hours of research and her unflagging commitment to me and to the project. It is, in every sense, her book, too.

It is also Lori Perkins' book. Ms. Perkins, my able agent, shepherded this book into print.

Heartfelt appreciation to Mr. Mike Wallace of CBS who agreed so readily to write a foreword. I am grateful for his decency and sensitivity during and after the filming of the *60 Minutes* segment.

Thanks also to my editor, Ms. Coleen O'Shea and her assistant, Beth Kugler, who were kind, tactful, intelligent, and consummately professional. And to Dave Cole for keen-eyed copyediting.

I am indebted to Ms. Joan Slighte, who typed much of the first draft manuscript, and Ms. Susan Perkins, who helped with research.

Dr. Dan Embree, Dr. Gus Pelletier, Dr. Archie McDonald, Dr. Helen Boese, and Dr. Alan Powers deserve thanks for their assistance.

Mr. George Cuomo is owed a debt I can never repay. Most of what I know about writing I learned from him.

I wish to thank my good friends Jim and Carolyn Davidson for their emotional support and enthusiasm.

Thanks, too, to my mother and father for encouragement and the impetus to change the title. And to my sister, Connie, whose excitement about the project often exceeded my own.

Love and appreciation to my daughters, Sionann and Kelly, who were tormented by test questions during the time this book was being written. Their suggestions, comments, and love were vital to getting the book done.

Finally, thanks to my many students over the last twenty years—To those who knew, and those who did not.

CONTENTS

EPIGRAPH

This is the great private problem of man: death as the loss of the self. But what is this self? It is the sum of everything we remember. Thus, what terrifies us about death is not the loss of the future, but the loss of the past. Forgetting is a form of death ever present within life. . . .

But forgetting is also the great problem of politics. When a big power wants to deprive a small country of its national consciousness it uses the method of *Organized forgetting*. . . . A nation which loses awareness of its past gradually loses its self. . . .

Totalitarianism . . . deprives people of memory and thus retools them into a nation of children. All totalitarianisms do this. And perhaps our entire technical age does this, with its cult of future, its cult of youth and childhood, its indifference to the past and mistrust of thought.

Milan Kundera
The Book of Laughter and Forgetting

INTRODUCTION

Back in 1987, I introduced a *60 MINUTES* segment with the unlikely title "Kurt Waldheim, Anchorman."

"This is not a story about the president of Austria who's been accused of complicity in war crimes," I began, "nor is it a story about the television business. Instead, it's a story about how poorly informed, how poorly educated a lot of Americans are. It's about what we do and do not know of things like geography and history, current affairs and literature."

The reason for the title of the piece? In a current affairs test given by *60 MINUTES* to some junior college students, it turned out that a remarkable number had only the vaguest idea who Kurt Waldheim was; and one student had indeed answered that Waldheim was a TV anchorman.

The *60 MINUTES* segment was triggered by my reading a "My Turn" piece in *Newsweek* magazine, written by one Jaime O'Neill, then a professor of English at South Puget Sound Community College in Olympia, Washington. O'Neill wrote about a test of general knowledge he had given his students, questions that covered a variety of subjects, essential and trivial. The results, I thought, were stunning—stunningly low.

60 MINUTES embarked on a similar test, with similar students at O'Neill's South Puget Sound, and the results were similarly discouraging. Our piece seemed to strike a nerve across America. We received hundreds of letters—letters of shame, letters of outrage, letters that said, in effect, that something must be missing in the American education system if we are turning out young adults with as sketchy a knowledge of fundamental facts as those test results seemed to indicate.

About a year later in Japan, we did another *60 MINUTES* piece, called "Head of the Class," about the Japanese system of education.

"Ninety-nine percent of the Japanese are literate," I said in introducing the segment. "In America, one of five Americans cannot even read the directions on how to change a tire or assemble a bicycle. And Japanese students consistently outscore Americans in reading and math, the basics."

It would seem the time has come to change that.

George Bush tells us he's going to be the "Education president," that he is determined that the level of training, knowledge, and understanding made available and dinned into young Americans is going to rise while he is in the White House.

Pray it is so.

Mike Wallace

PROLOGUE: HOW THIS BOOK CAME TO BE

Human history becomes more and more a race between education and catastrophe.

H. G. Wells

Knowledge is a state or condition of mind; and since cultivation of mind is surely worth seeking for its own sake, we are thus brought once more to the conclusion that there is a Knowledge, which is desirable, though nothing come of it, as being of itself a treasure, and a sufficient remuneration of years of labor.

Cardinal Newman

It seems ironic that out of the millions of teachers in this country, I should be one to publish a book of tests. In twenty years of teaching, I have never given an "objective" test, at least not one that would count toward a grade. The fact is, I don't much believe in them. They skew the aims of education, corrupt students, and distort the purpose of learning. Tests have come to outweigh teaching and learning, becoming more important than either of those activities, short-circuiting the process and establishing intimidation and implied but abstract reward as spurious motivators for the acquisition of skills and knowledge. Although no one probably intended it this way, learning frequently ceases once the tests have been given, the scores tabulated, the records kept.

Learning should begin *after* the tests have been given. It is my hope that anyone who might use this book will use it as a tool to define areas for further exploration.

And that is how this book came to be. After years of assigning and reading the most vapid of student research papers on subjects of current controversy, I decided to return to an outmoded and discredited teaching exercise—the simple report, where students gather knowledge, then assimilate that knowledge by writing about it. Because I suspected that students were hungering for content, that they were often bewildered by classroom references or allusions to things I took to be common knowledge, I contrived an eighty-six-question quiz of people, places, and events I assumed were widely and generally known. The idea was that students would take the quiz, diagnose their areas of ignorance, then go to the library to fill in those gaps by gathering information and assimilating that information through the process of writing about it. Then they could say yes to anyone who might ask if they had learned anything in school that day. Here was an exercise in which students could go directly from not knowing to knowing. Since much education these days is based on skills, students can take precious little sense of accomplishment or achievement from their labors because skills grow slowly and progress is difficult to assess, but the acquisition of knowledge is more tangible and its rewards more immediate. Learn a new word and you can use it immediately, but a 10 percent improvement in your backhand will still leave you missing shots. "What did you learn in school today?" is how the question goes. "Nothin' much," is the nearly inevitable answer.

I expected that students would miss no more than five or six questions and would, in turn, do five or six short reports, with bibliographies. When the results came in, however, I found that most students had missed more than half of the questions. I could not ask them to prepare forty or fifty brief research papers—or, in some cases, eighty-six research papers.

Since the publishing of my test results a dozen studies have been conducted, all of which verify my rather dismal findings. Almost anything one might have thought to be common knowledge proves to be far less commonly known than supposed.

Is it important? Does it matter? I am one who thinks that it is important, that it does matter. Much of the ignorance is willful; it is a choice we have made, individually or collectively. If the past does not matter, how can the future matter? If, quite literally, we don't know where we are (many Americans cannot locate the United States on a blank map of the world), how then can we possibly know where we are going?

All teachers know that part of their job requires salesmanship. Before we can teach students, we must first sell them on the value of our wares. Perhaps this should not be so, but it is so. The current social and cultural atmosphere in the United States makes promises of material reward the most effective sales pitch for knowing and learning. If a teacher can demonstrate the dollar value of what is being taught, students will be interested and pay attention. But even this pitch doesn't work all the time. Students are terrifically resourceful at imagining careers requiring nothing but the narrowest of skills and abilities. Writing can be discounted: "I'll have a secretary to do that." History is easily dismissed: "So what? Who needs the past? We're looking at the future." Current events and politics? "Who cares? Can't do nothin' about it anyway."

So, after all those years of often poor salesmanship to an increasingly indifferent clientele, it came to me that there is really only one sales presentation worth making. That sales idea is that it is better to know than not to know, better to press back our ignorance in whatever small ways we can than to accept it as our inevitable condition.

And I'm not much concerned with the squabbles currently being conducted over *what* is good to know. Sorting out what is essential, significant, and enduring is important, surely. But deciding which pieces of information are most important is best left to individual learners, who are best able to make those judgments only after they've learned a great welter of things. Is it more important to know who Socrates was, or to know the ideas for which he is remembered? It seems a foolish question. The fact is, it is difficult, if not impossible, to know one without the other. Is it important to know about Ethel Mertz, or is Ethel Rosenberg more important? One must know about both before making a distinction.

And making distinctions is one of the important things knowledge allows us to do. Recently I watched a woman spend an increasingly frustrating hour in a bookstore. She wanted very much to buy a book, something engaging and stimulating to read, but she was bewildered by the titles and the names of the authors. She could not, in fact, distinguish one from the other. She was bored with television and wanted to exercise her mind, but she left the bookstore without making a purchase. She simply had no way to decide what was likely to prove interesting and what was not.

Yes, there are relative levels of significance, seriousness, and importance, but I would not like to have those choices made by any agency, committee, or forum I can imagine. Culture is vital and nearly organic in that it grows out of need and usage. Writers who were not included in the standard anthologies and textbooks twenty years ago are now resurrected in response to social, cultural, and critical changes. Historical episodes, half forgotten, are retrieved when corollaries are discovered in today's events. Scholars resuscitate interest with new findings and new information. The widest possible spread of knowledge will be our best protection from some uniform, encoded, and limited edict about what is important and what is not. Ultimately, people should be well enough informed and well enough educated to make those choices. Uninformed or ill-informed, they make those choices anyway.

The tests that make up the bulk of this book are intended only to measure a small bit of what you know and what you don't know. What is being tested is limited and fairly arbitrary. No claim is made that the knowledge tested in this book even approaches comprehensiveness. Humanities and the liberal arts tradition are emphasized over scientific knowledge. Cultural biases toward Western culture are implicit, not because Western culture is superior, but because it is the culture we live in. Popular culture is given rather large measure because it finds its way into so much of what we read and talk about. The tests in this book might try your memory, or the efficacy of your education, but these tests are not meant to assess your intelligence, your ability to think clearly, or your value as a human being.

The tests are, however, meant to point out *ignorance*, a word that, when properly understood, loses its negative connotation. To be ignorant is only to be human. As the saying goes, "The more you know, the more you know you don't know." Ignorance may not be bliss, but it is the human condition. We need not be stupid about it, however. Admitting ignorance allows us to get on with the business of knowing, of reducing in whatever small way we can the sum total of all that we don't know.

We are awash in information, with more flooding in at us all the time. How do we stay afloat in this deluge? Commentators in both the print and broadcast media are fond of telling us that the "knowledge base" is doubling every five years, or five minutes. There are some ninety thousand new books published each year, compared to eight thousand in 1950. There are nearly a million books in print, compared to some eighty-five thousand in 1950. So it would seem that the world is a more knowledgeable place than it was forty years ago, and that the challenges of knowing and being well informed are ten times more demanding now than then.

But we can increase our buoyancy in these waters if we are reminded that this knowledge base is often made up of very specialized knowledge, that these thousands of volumes include much that is redundant, much that is truly trivial. Included in that count of ninety thousand new books, for example, are some nineteen cookbooks instructing people on how to cook with soybeans.

If a task seems too formidable, it is likely to *be* too formidable for those who have that impression. Daunted by the sheer volume of knowledge, or the supposed volume of knowledge, many of us simply give up, look to the commercial diversions and distractions that are designed to capture our time and attention.

And attention is hard to come by in a society like ours. We are programmed to have shorter and shorter attention spans. Radio cannot abide a silence, a pause for thought or reflection. Television cannot allow the eye to rest on anything for longer than six seconds. As we become more passive, other people decide for us just where attention should be focused—and for how long. Reclaiming our own attention is one of the gifts of knowledge. Knowing things can give us back a piece of ourselves.

Most of the tests in this book are the product of a kind of free association. Once the category was established, names, events, places, titles, or ideas would begin to suggest themselves to me. One idea would inevitably prompt two or three more. Sometimes the connections were clear and I could see how or why one name or event would suggest another. But just as often, the connections and associations were murky and mysterious. Why, for instance, did the name Margaret Mead evoke the name of Frank Buck? Why did Woody Allen remind me of the House Un-American Activities Committee?

However mysterious, this is how thinking gets done. We are not computers. Each of us processes information differently. The way facts and names and dates connect in our minds tells us as much about ourselves as individuals as the facts tell about the world we live in. To learn facts, to gather information, is to engage in a kind of self-discovery. Facts are never impersonal. We make of them what we will; we make of them what we are, and what they make us become.

It is my hope, then, that you will make these tests your own and—after discovering what you know and don't know—will pick and choose what is significant and relevant to you. I hope teachers might use the tests to give students direction in their learning. In any list of inert facts it is possible to find something that might explain or illuminate a corner of your life, enhance a piece of your understanding. It came as a great surprise to me at one point in my education to learn that there wasn't always a Pentagon. The fact that things were not always as they are is a greatly liberating and stimulating thing to know.

It's all good to know. Knowing things, trivial or otherwise, makes the world a more varied and interesting place. Knowing things extends your ability to imagine what is possible. What would you readily give up knowing? What bit of information attached to your body of knowledge would you renounce? The human mind is often compared to an attic. People who make this analogy seem to suggest that, if we could, it would be a good idea to clean out the attic once in a while to make room for new and improved knowledge. But while forgetting is a most real phenomenon, it is not one we control. Even if we could, I wouldn't want the job of choosing what to discard. Surely, just as soon as I decided I could easily get along without knowing that e. e. cummings' initials stood for Edward Estlin, the very next day I would be certain to find a use for that admittedly arcane bit of information. Just as soon as I decided I could get along nicely, thank you, without knowing that Tarzan had a chimp named Cheetah, surely along would come some reference or allusion or joke to make me blink uncomprehendingly.

So, as part of our sojourn on this planet, we acquire and stockpile what we know. If we manage to stay alive and alert to the world, our knowledge grows and that knowledge makes us more interested and interesting. In these "no-fault" tests, you can make the briefest assessment of what has adhered to you during your own sojourn here. And, if you find there are things you don't know that compel your interest or curiosity, you can begin the process of finding out and filling in. The very fact that you hold this book in your hand suggests that curiosity remains alive in you.

I should add a few words about scoring. It is difficult to justify a scoring mechanism of any kind in a book that claims to be a "no-fault" test of knowledge. Unless all readers score a hundred percent on all the tests, scoring itself implies fault-finding, conveys the message that one is not all that one should be.

But having no scoring mechanism would be like playing tennis without a net—a more successful way to play the game, to be sure, but also less interesting and rewarding.

So the scoring mechanisms that follow the answers at the end of each chapter are meant to bring up the level of your game, to give you a crude and sometimes fairly arbitrary self-assessment. Whatever your scores, you should keep in mind that the purpose of the scoring is diagnostic, not recriminatory. If your scores disappoint you, they should be interpreted only as a prod toward bringing up your game.

CHAPTER ONE

THE *60 MINUTES* TEST

I know you, at least a little bit. You are outwardly confident, as gregarious as you need to be, apparently well informed, eager to please. Beneath that outward appearance, there is someone else lurking, however, someone who is not so confident, not so self-assured, not so well informed. This hidden you is, in part, the creation of an educational system unwittingly constructed to make you this way, a system that has convinced you your worth and value are directly proportional to how much you know, then failed to acquaint you with very much of that knowledge.

If you dropped out of school, you have spent part of your life apologizing for that fact, or you've been busy for years defensively crying out against the "educated fools." Even if you've earned advanced degrees, you harbor the suspicion that your education was narrow, overly specialized, inadequate to the diversity of knowledge the world at large bombards you with every day.

You hear the news when walking through a room. Important things are happening somewhere in the world, events unfolding that might have an impact on your own life. The places are far off, mysteriously located somewhere out there. The issues are cloudy, fragmented, communicated in 60-, 90-, 120-second bites accompanied by meaningless pictures of people in places that may or may not look familiar.

"The World is too much with us," Wordsworth (Who? Most college students wouldn't know) wrote in the nineteenth century. Nearly two hundred years later, it is more with us than ever, despite our best efforts to tune it out.

Recently I gave a presentation to a civic group. Afterwards, a man came up to take the test you are about to take in this first chapter. As so often happens, he wanted to take it orally, in my presence. Someone, you see, needed to be present to validate what he knew, to establish what his experiential and scholastic educations had failed to establish: that he was okay, suitably knowledgeable, admitted to the club. As he went down the list of names, events, and places, he would identify those things he knew. All other questions were answered with the phrase "Not important." This was an inventive, but typical, adaptation to insecurities about what we know and don't know. Paul Simon has a song entitled "I Know What I Know." We all know what we know, but we secretly suspect that it's not enough.

Teachers are accustomed to hearing students limit their aspirations. What students want out of an education, quite commonly, is "enough to get by." The problem, for them and for the institutions that teach them, is that no one seems to know just what constitutes "enough," and fewer still know what it means to "get by." Does it mean the simple ability to pass your days, to perform a repetitive task, to earn a living? Or might it mean something like casting off the fetters of a life viewed too narrowly, a perspective shrunk too close to the nose? Does "getting by" in your present circumstances ensure that you will get by in a world rife with change? And can accumulating facts and data and places and names ensure getting by in any case?

These are all heady questions, the usual handwringing done when someone in the media wishes to attract attention, stir action, add to the public's vast worry pile. But this needn't be so fraught with weight and worry. The central contention of this book is that it is *Good to Know*, better to know than not to know. Knowledge begets knowledge, and in the words of the old axiom, knowledge is power. It is well and good to know and understand modern psychoanalysis, to arrive at your own conclusions about it, but if that understanding is expressed while pronouncing Freud as "Frood," then the power is, at the very least, diminished. It is well and good to be a patriot, but that patriotism is less likely to be abused by politicians or misguided by misunderstanding if you truly know our national heritage and rise above slogans and symbols.

So what is essential to know? Most of us have only a vague answer to that question. Scholars and teachers can't agree. Let's see what you think.

Would you expect American college students to routinely know who Adolph Eichmann was? In a sampling drawn from five hundred students in colleges in eleven states, 82.4 percent did not know of Eichmann. Important? Should we expect succeeding generations to remember him, to know of his trial, of his significance, of his misdeeds and their implications?

Or how about Ho Chi Minh? The sons and daughters (and brothers and sisters, in some cases) of men who fought the Ho Chi Minh regime are 69 percent ignorant of who he was. Does it matter?

Gdansk? It's nearly always in the news, but three out of four of the five hundred college students tested had no idea where it is. So what?

The Magna Carta? "What's that?" according to 85 percent of the students tested.

Waterloo? 62 percent couldn't tell when the battle happened within a hundred years.

More than half were ignorant of Appomattox.

Sixty-two percent did not know what NAACP stands for.

Sixty-eight percent were unaware of SDI.

Sixty-six percent hadn't heard about the Moral Majority; more than one in three don't know what a Nazi is; nearly two out of three had not heard and understood the term *Yuppie*.

Nearly half did not know who wrote *King Lear*, by any measure one of the crowning literary achievements of Western culture. Nearly 80 percent did not know who wrote *Moby-Dick*, the epic American novel some critics define as the most American book ever written.

And, for a society awash in media religion for the last decade, it is surprising that 85 percent had no idea who wrote the Book of Genesis; that nearly four out of ten don't know when Christ was born.

But perhaps it isn't surprising. Part of our terror about our own ignorance has to do with the fact that no one seems to know what should be expected—either of ourselves or of others. What should newspeople know? Politicians know? Voters know? It is fairly clear that if there is such a thing as common knowledge, it's rather unclear what that knowledge might be. What can be said about a culture and about a country when there is little commonly shared knowledge about anything? What happens to the process of communication? To education? To our politics and public discourse?

Let's sample what that fragmentation and ignorance produce. Taken from the incorrect answers given by a small sampling of students, I've compiled a new history of the world, a pastiche of misunderstanding and confusion, the world according to ignorance. Here is revisionist history even George Orwell (unknown to multitudes of college students) could not have invented. From three American college classrooms of the 1980s, here is a brave old world (allusion: Huxley, also little remembered) constructed from what those students "knew" about their heritage and their planet.

THE WORLD ACCORDING TO IGNORANCE

A long time ago, in the seventeenth century, Christ was born. At that time, Dwight Eisenhower was president of the United States, but he often took vacations at Camp David in Israel near Christ's birthplace. In fact, a lot of stuff was happening around this time. For instance, Charles Darwin invented gravity, which made a lot of people more down-to-earth. This invention was quite popular, as revealed by the Gallup "poles." Meanwhile, in Rio de Janeiro in France, Napoleon, a Russian, was planning to invade Leningrad, Germany. About this same time, Andy Warhol was writing his masterpiece, *War and Peace*, from his home in Stratford-upon-Avon, Germany.

Time passed and got more modern. J. Edgar Hoover, an early U.S. president and communist, enjoyed the music of composer Arthur Miller, cheered baseball players Woody Guthrie and Ralph Nader, and became a disciple of Karl Marx, the famous Russian comedian who wrote *Mein Kampf*. Some people disagreed with Hoover and thought he was suffering from Alzheimer's disease, which had been recently discovered by Kurt Waldheim, who also served as a TV anchorman. Meanwhile, an aging Charles Darwin continued his work and added to his invention of gravity the achievement of discovering the theory of "evaluation." J. Edgar Hoover, in retirement, invented the vacuum cleaner. Not long after, Heinrich Himmler, a firefighter who wrote music, invented the Heimlich maneuver. Himmler was a native of Calcutta, New Mexico, who loved ravioli, which Antonio Vivaldi had invented. Meanwhile, President Joseph McCarthy wrote *The Red Badge of Courage* and took a trip to Florence, France, in hopes of getting a glimpse of Pablo Picasso's "The Last Supper." At about this time, Columbus set out for the New World, which helped to touch off the American Revolution in either the fourteenth century, or the 1860s. Benito Mussolini, who composed music, painted pictures, and designed great cathedrals, relaxed by following the exploits of Albert Schweitzer, a famous weight lifter of that time. Schweitzer, who lived a long life thanks to his commitment to physical fitness, later became Secretary of the Navy, serving on the cabinet with Kurt Waldheim, Secretary of Defense. This administration suffered scandal when Secretary of State Winston Churchill, a French comedian, later became the leader of Nazi Germany, commanding his country from the capital city of Belfast.

The Silver War struck the United States, pitting brother

against brother, North against South. Francis Scott Key wrote "'The Battle Hymn of the Republic," which was a pop song in those days until the war was settled during peace talks in Geneva, Canada.

On the lighter side, Vincent van Gogh, actor, portrayed F. Scott Fitzgerald, president, in the first stage version of *Uncle Tom's Cabin* by Geoffrey Chaucer. Chaucer, who had also served as prime minister of England, where Tripoli is located, put another noted actor, Henry Ford, in the cast. Henry Ford and Vincent van Gogh were theatrical sensations as they toured with Chaucer's play, appearing in such cities as Belfast, Belgium; Dresden, England; Nagasaki, Vietnam; Beirut, Iran; and Copenhagen, Canada. Jonas Salk, noted Russian leader, welcomed them personally when they appeared in Barcelona, Russia.

More time passed and many people were confused about what direction it was going. Norman Rockwell, well-known crook and founder of Rockwell International, was convicted and shared a cell with Andy Warhol, Jewish leader and political prisoner who had, of course, written *War and Peace* many years earlier. It was a time of turmoil as the twentieth century approached. Sigmund Freud, the "nut," was immortalized by film producer Herman Melville. The century whipped by, giving rise to Prince, who wrote *The Color Purple* from his home in Capetown, Connecticut. Timothy Leary joined President Reagan's cabinet as Secretary of Defense. And the rest, of course, is history.

This much ignorance, and more, was afoot in those three classrooms. Although no one on the planet holds precisely this view of history and geography, a great many people—many with college degrees—hold a view of the world just as fragmented, just as incoherent. How does one speak to such an audience? Distributed over a nation in which three out of four don't attend college at all, what assumptions might be made about the failures of the educational enterprise, about "collective unconsciousness," about the ocean of ignorance through which we try to navigate a national dialogue?

These inventive wrong answers are not provided so that we might sneer and jibe. Some of the processes that directed students to such inspired flights of creative guesswork are easy to see. Ill-equipped, but eager to please, they gave it their best shot; in doing so, they made stunningly wrong choices—which is, after all, how it will go in the absence of knowledge. Although knowing a great many things has precious little to do with innate intelligence, it has a great deal to do with the *perception* of innate intelligence.

Although there is a serious social and cultural problem when so many people fail to know so much, it is worth remembering, in a world of problems and crises, that human beings are fragile and fallible, and there has always been humor in that fallibility. When we laugh at these wildly wrong answers, these woefully gained misperceptions, we laugh at ourselves.

And sometimes the laugh catches in our throats.

In the aftermath of the American Revolution (only one in three high school students know that the Declaration of Independence was the document that declared the thirteen colonies independent of England), a forgotten writer expressed an unsurprising and commonly held opinion. He wrote:

> *From public schools shall general knowledge flow,*
> *For 'tis the people's sacred right—to know.*

This was the faith of our forefathers (and mothers). Have we kept faith with their faith?

The test you are about to take—the first of a series of such tests in this book—won't require an hour of your time. It's called the *60 MINUTES* test because it was featured on a *60 MINUTES* segment in which Mike Wallace exposed and lamented the broad ignorance of today's college student. Since that program aired, this test has been administered in over a thousand high schools, colleges, universities, offices, factories, prisons, and service clubs and associations. No matter where the test is given, it always produces the same dismaying results.

America, more than any other industrialized nation, seems to be losing touch with who it is, where it is, where it came from. We forget, apparently, our heroes and our hallowed ground. We misplace entire continents, discard our past like worn-out shoes, reinvent history as we go along, improvising a heritage from half-remembered and ill-digested scraps of folklore and television sound bites. Meanwhile, the educators squabble among themselves about what deserves to be incorporated into the education of our young.

Such forgetfulness and indifference come with a price, of course. "Knowledge is the ruination of my young troops," said Adolf Hitler in the late 1930s. Today in America there are college graduates who can only guess at who Hitler was, who are not able to define what the Holocaust was, who know nothing of their grandfathers' war. And while they don't know these things, some of their teachers and professors argue that such ignorance is benign, that it is, after all, more important to turn out graduates who can compute and perform technocratic skills, or who can "think critically" in the absence of a context in which that thinking can take place. Others argue that Western culture is sexist and racist and therefore unworthy of perpetuation. Still others assert that the new computer memory storage technology frees us of the need to know history, literature, geography, and current events. If we find that we need to know something, they argue, we can push a button and call it up, or at the very least go somewhere and look it up.

But it won't wash. Common knowledge is an important aspect of conversation and social cohesion, and knowing things feels better than not knowing things. Knowing things *informs* us, individually and collectively, gives us shape and identity.

So now it's your turn. Take this test and compare your score with the average. If you're a parent, have your kids take the test. What you know might surprise you. What you don't know (and what others don't know) might surprise you even more. Parenthetical percentages at the right of each question indicate how many students in a five-hundred-student sample did not know.

ESSENTIAL OR TRIVIAL:
A Test of General Knowledge

PART I. IDENTIFY THE FOLLOWING PEOPLE. WHO WERE THEY? WHEN DID THEY LIVE?

1. Albert Schweitzer .... (83.4% incorrect)
2. J. Edgar Hoover........................ (58.2% incorrect)
3. Charles Dickens........................ (86.1% incorrect)
4. Joseph McCarthy .... (77.8% incorrect)
5. Johann Sebastian Bach................. (26.8% incorrect)
6. Spiro Agnew........................... (86.3% incorrect)
7. Karl Marx............................. (49.4% incorrect)
8. James Joyce .... (91% incorrect)
9. Kurt Waldheim .... (73% incorrect)
10. Jimmy Hoffa.......................... (84.1% incorrect)
11. Robert Frost .... (26.4% incorrect)
12. Norman Mailer .... (68.3% incorrect)
13. Jonas Salk .... (65.4% incorrect)
14. Ansel Adams .... (78.4% incorrect)

15. Francis Scott Key . . . . (94% incorrect)

16. Virginia Woolf . . . . (90.2% incorrect)

17. Norman Rockwell . . . . (56.1% incorrect)

18. Albert Einstein. (54.2% incorrect)

19. Charles Darwin. . . . . (31% incorrect)

20. Andy Warhol . . . . (67.6% incorrect)

21. Ray Kroc . . . . (78% incorrect)

22. Mohandas Gandhi . . . . (60.4% incorrect)

23. Ho Chi Minh . . . . (68.8% incorrect)

24. Ralph Nader . . . . (76.5% incorrect)

25. Sigmund Freud. (22.6% incorrect)

26. George Gallup . . . . (72.4% incorrect)

27. Timothy Leary . . . . (38% incorrect)

28. Jefferson Davis . . . . (55.2% incorrect)

29. Benito Mussolini . . . . (50.5% incorrect)

30. Pablo Picasso . . . . (15.8% incorrect)

31. F. Scott Fitzgerald . . . . (55% incorrect)

32. Vincent van Gogh . . . . (53.8% incorrect)

33. Steven Spielberg. (4.1% incorrect)

34. Herman Melville . . . . (60.2% incorrect)

35. Babe Ruth. . . . . (3.2% incorrect)

36. Dwight Eisenhower . . . . (54.8% incorrect)

37. Henry Ford . . . . (28.1% incorrect)

38. John Hancock. . . . . (34.8% incorrect)

39. Samuel Clemens . . . . (61.2% incorrect)

40. Benjamin Franklin. . . . . (24.8% incorrect)

41. Geoffrey Chaucer. . . . . (50.8% incorrect)

42. Winston Churchill. . . . . (24.4% incorrect)

43. William Tecumseh Sherman . . . . (81% incorrect)

44. Arthur Miller . . . . (84% incorrect)

45. Woody Guthrie . . . . (78% incorrect)

46. Ethel Rosenberg . . . . (87% incorrect)

47. Jack Benny . . . . (60.2% incorrect)

48. Charles Manson . . . . (18% incorrect)

49. Adolf Eichmann . . . . (82.4% incorrect)
50. Napoleon Bonaparte . . . . (35.6% incorrect)

PART II. IN WHAT COUNTRIES ARE THE FOLLOWING PLACES LOCATED?

51. Alamogordo . . . . (80.4% incorrect)
52. Florence . . . . (51% incorrect)
53. Nagasaki . . . . (48% incorrect)
54. Rio de Janeiro . . . . (68.5% incorrect)
55. Dresden . . . . (73.6% incorrect)
56. Melbourne . . . . (65.2% incorrect)
57. Capetown . . . . (74.6% incorrect)
58. Calcutta . . . . (49% incorrect)
59. Tripoli . . . . (72.6% incorrect)
60. Versailles . . . . (79% incorrect)
61. Havana . . . . (27.8% incorrect)
62. Kiev . . . . (44.8% incorrect)
63. Belfast . . . . (55.6% incorrect)
64. Quebec . . . . (13.4% incorrect)
65. Geneva . . . . (42% incorrect)
66. Beirut . . . . (38.2% incorrect)
67. Seoul . . . . (21.4% incorrect)
68. Bogotá . . . . (88.6% incorrect)
69. Leningrad . . . . (22.2% incorrect)
70. Barcelona . . . . (70.1% incorrect)
71. Managua . . . . (59% incorrect)
72. Camp David . . . . (61.2% incorrect)
73. Copenhagen . . . . (53.6% incorrect)
74. Gdansk . . . . (75.4% incorrect)
75. Stratford-upon-Avon . . . . (71.4% incorrect)

PART III. WHO WERE THE AUTHORS OF THE FOLLOWING?

76. *Huckleberry Finn* . . . . (23.2% incorrect)
77. *Uncle Tom's Cabin* . . . . (66% incorrect)
78. *King Lear* . . . . (47.6% incorrect)
79. *The Color Purple* . . . . (87.4% incorrect)
80. *The Great Gatsby* . . . . (63.6% incorrect)
81. *War and Peace* . . . . (73.4% incorrect)

PART IV. IDENTIFY
THE FOLLOWING.
WHAT DO THE
INITIALS STAND FOR?

PART V. IN WHAT
CENTURIES DID THE
FOLLOWING EVENTS
TAKE PLACE?

82. The Declaration of Independence . . . . (31% incorrect)

83. The Gettysburg Address . . . . (22.2% incorrect)

84. FBI. . . . . (31.4% incorrect)

85. IRS. . . . . ~. . . . . (10.4% incorrect)

86. CIA . . . . (39.2% incorrect)

87. *Yuppies* . . . . (58.2% incorrect)

88. The Cuban Missile Crisis. . . . . (17.4% incorrect)

89. Appomattox . . . . (50.8% incorrect)

90. Waterloo . . . . (62.2% incorrect)

91. Columbus' voyage to the New World . . . . (35.6% incorrect)

92. The American Revolution. . . . . (31.4% incorrect)

93. Hiroshima . . . . (20.4% incorrect)

94. The Battle of the Little Bighorn . . . . (41.6% incorrect)

95. The birth of Christ . . . . (37.2% incorrect)

96. The French Revolution . . . . (57.8% incorrect)

97. The Magna Charta . . . . (85% incorrect)

98. The Golden Age of Television . . . . (29% incorrect)

99. The Emancipation Proclamation. . . . . (42% incorrect)

100. Sputnik. . . . . (48.6% incorrect)

To check how well you did, refer to the answers provided at the end of this chapter.

Is this test definitive? Does it establish a base of "common knowledge"? Is every question significant? Surely not, but most of the questions are the sorts of things you might encounter in reading, in conversation, even on television.

Many people have dismissed tests of this kind as trivial, of importance only to eggheads, crossword puzzlers, game show contestants. But if you've ever been caught in your ignorance, felt the embarrassment of not knowing what everyone else seemed to know, then you know that not knowing is hardly trivial. In fact, the word *trivial* is tossed about as though it means "unimportant." The literal meaning of the word, however, refers to things you are likely to encounter every day. If allusions and references are bombarding you, and if you're deprived of knowledge about them, your self-esteem is bound to suffer, your self-confidence sure to decline.

ANSWERS

1. Albert Schweitzer (1875–1965)—French Protestant clergyman, philosopher, and physician

2. J. Edgar Hoover (1895–1972)—director of the Federal Bureau of Investigation, 1924–1972

3. Charles Dickens (1812–1870)—English novelist whose works include *Oliver Twist, David Copperfield, A Christmas Carol, Great Expectations,* and *A Tale of Two Cities*

4. Joseph McCarthy (1908–1957)—Senator from Wisconsin who in the 1950s attacked those he considered communist

5. Johann Sebastian Bach (1685–1750)—German composer and organist

6. Spiro Agnew (1918–)—vice president under Richard Nixon, resigned in 1973 after being accused of accepting bribes

7. Karl Marx (1818–1883)—German social philosopher and chief theorist of modern socialism and communism

8. James Joyce (1882–1941)—Irish novelist whose works include *Ulysses*

9. Kurt Waldheim (1918–)—Austrian president, secretary general of United Nations, 1972–1981

10. Jimmy Hoffa (1913–disappeared 1975)—U.S. labor leader, president of Teamsters Union, 1957–1971, convicted of jury tampering and fraud in handling of union benefits fund

11. Robert Frost (1874–1963)—American poet

12. Norman Mailer (1923–)—American writer whose works include *The Naked and the Dead*

13. Jonas Salk (1914–)—American physician and microbiologist known for his work in developing a vaccine for polio

14. Ansel Adams (1902–1984)—American photographer known for landscapes, especially Yosemite Valley and High Sierra

15. Francis Scott Key (1779–1843)—American lawyer and poet who wrote "The Star-Spangled Banner"

16. Virginia Woolf (1882–1941)—English novelist and essayist

17. Norman Rockwell (1894–1978)—American illustrator known best for his covers for the *Saturday Evening Post*

18. Albert Einstein (1879–1955)—American physicist born in Germany who developed the theory of relativity

19. Charles Darwin (1809–1882)—English naturalist known for his theory of evolution

20. Andy Warhol (1930–1987)—American artist and filmmaker, leading exponent of pop art movement

21. Ray Kroc (1902–1984)—Builder of McDonald's fast-food empire

22. Mohandas Gandhi (1869–1943)—Indian political and spiritual leader

23. Ho Chi Minh (1890–1969)—Vietnamese nationalist leader, president of North Vietnam, 1954–1969

24. Ralph Nader (1934–)—American lawyer and consumer advocate

25. Sigmund Freud (1850–1939)—Austrian psychiatrist who was the founder of psychoanalysis

26. George Gallup (1901–1984)—American public opinion statistician who established the Gallup Poll

27. Timothy Leary (1920–)—American psychologist and author known for his experimentation with hallucinogenic drugs in the 1960s

28. Jefferson Davis (1808–1889)—American statesman, president of Confederate States of America

29. Benito Mussolini (1883–1945)—Italian dictator and leader of the Fascist movement

30. Pablo Picasso (1881–1973)—Spanish painter, sculptor, and graphic artist, one of the foremost figures in twentieth century art

31. F. Scott Fitzgerald (1896–1940)—American novelist and short-story writer whose works include *The Great Gatsby*

32. Vincent van Gogh (1853–1890)—Dutch post-impressionist painter

33. Steven Spielberg (1947–)—American movie director whose films include *Jaws, Close Encounters of the Third Kind, E.T.,* and *Raiders of the Lost Ark*

34. Herman Melville (1819–1891)—American author best known for *Moby-Dick*

35. Babe Ruth (1895–1948)—American baseball player

36. Dwight Eisenhower (1890–1969)—American general and thirty-fourth president of the United States

37. Henry Ford (1863–1947)—American industrialist, pioneer auto manufacturer; adopted assembly line methods to auto production

38. John Hancock (1737–1793)—political leader during the American Revolution; famous for his large signature on the Declaration of Independence

39. Samuel Clemens (1835–1910)—American author and satirist who wrote under the pen name Mark Twain; works included *The Celebrated Jumping Frog of Calaveras County, and Other Sketches; The Adventures of Huckleberry Finn; The Adventures of Tom Sawyer;* and much more

40. Benjamin Franklin (1706–1790)—American statesman, printer, scientist, and writer; wrote and published *Poor Richard's Almanack* (1732–1757) under the pseudonym Richard Saunders

41. Geoffrey Chaucer (ca. 1340–1400)—English poet. *The Canterbury Tales* was his masterpiece

42. Winston Churchill (1874–1965)—British statesman, soldier, author. Prime minister of England during World War II

43. William Tecumseh Sherman (1820–1891)—Union general during the Civil War. Known for destructive Atlanta campaign and the "March to the Sea" in Georgia

44. Arthur Miller (1915–)—American dramatist. Works include *Death of a Salesman* and *The Crucible*

45. Woody Guthrie (1912–1967)—American folksinger and composer. Wrote the song "This Land Is Your Land"

46. Ethel Rosenberg (1916–1953)—Indicted with her husband, Julius, for conspiring to transmit classified military information to the Soviet Union in the early 1950s; found guilty and executed in 1953

47. Jack Benny (1894–1974)—American comedian and entertainer

48. Charles Manson (1934–)—infamous leader of a "family" who killed seven people in the Tate-LaBianca murders in August 1969

49. Adolf Eichmann (1906–1962)—German Nazi, advocated the use of gas chambers to exterminate Jews in concentration camps; was hanged in Israel for crimes against Jews and humanity

50. Napoleon Bonaparte (1769–1821)—French emperor

51. Alamagordo, New Mexico, the site of the explosion of the first atomic bomb on July 16, 1945

52. Florence, Italy

53. Nagasaki, Japan, the second city to be hit by an atomic bomb in Japan in World War II

54. Rio de Janeiro, Brazil

55. Dresden, East Germany

56. Melbourne, Australia

57. Capetown, South Africa

58. Calcutta, India

59. One Tripoli is the capital of Libya, another is a city in Lebanon

60. Versailles, France

61. Havana, Cuba

62. Kiev, Soviet Union

63. Belfast, Northern Ireland

64. Quebec, Canada

65. Geneva, Switzerland

66. Beirut, Lebanon

67. Seoul, South Korea

68. Bogotá, Colombia

69. Leningrad, Soviet Union

70. Barcelona, Spain

71. Managua, Nicaragua

72. Camp David, Maryland, United States

73. Copenhagen, Denmark

74. Gdansk, Poland

75. Stratford-upon-Avon, England

76. Mark Twain

77. Harriet Beecher Stowe

78. William Shakespeare

79. Alice Walker

80. F. Scott Fitzgerald

81. Leo Tolstoy

82. Thomas Jefferson was the principal author

83. Abraham Lincoln

84. Federal Bureau of Investigation

85. Internal Revenue Service

86. Central Intelligence Agency

87. Young urban professionals

88. Twentieth century

89. Nineteenth century

90. Nineteenth century

91. Fifteenth century

92. Eighteenth century

93. Twentieth century

94. Nineteenth century

95. First century

96. Eighteenth century

97. Thirteenth century

98. Twentieth century

99. Nineteenth century

100. Twentieth century

SCORING

You've probably already provided yourself with an assessment of your knowledge of the items in this test by comparing what you knew with the percentage of students who didn't know. If not, you can measure your results against the following:

71–100: You have an uncommonly good grasp of common knowledge.

41–70: Your score is consistent with average scores achieved by college students around the country.

31–40: While there is much you know, there is much you might wish to know.

30 or less: You have serious deficiencies in your stock of common knowledge.

CHAPTER TWO

REALITY CHECK

One of the greatest gifts of knowledge is the ability to make distinctions. What we know allows us to draw distinctions between historical periods, artists, writers, politicians, generals and composers.

Perhaps the simplest distinction we can draw is between what is real and what is imagined. This chapter tests your ability to make that distinction.

Perhaps the test in the first chapter strengthened your confidence, perhaps not. That is the way of tests. Since the American educational system seems more concerned with testing than with teaching, most people who progress through twelve or more years of such "education" are, in effect, brutalized. They are constantly forced to put their self-image, self-confidence, and self-esteem on the line. As a means of self-protection, many people decide that none of it matters very much, that it's all "academic," set apart from the real world, unimportant. Or, if they have a history of doing well on tests and mastering the art of test taking, they then sometimes become insufferable—bores and know-it-alls who are routinely ostracized by other students.

If we had contrived to construct a system to make knowing things onerous and unpalatable, we could hardly have done a better job.

But however badly the educational system is doing in convincing students that it is important to know things, knowing things is still an important survival skill, a significant component of vital self-esteem.

The test you are about to take is probably more difficult than the test in Chapter One. Many of the items are more obscure, but each leads to further learning, to means of making connections between the many and varied elements of human history and experience. Facts and knowledge, it seems, provide a way of anchoring our reality, of taking the fragmented world and making it somewhat more whole and coherent.

Without some degree of common knowledge, coherence is hard to come by. Without coherence, the world is mad. One common definition of insanity is the inability to distinguish between reality and fantasy, between what we imagine and what we know is true. We've heard stories about people who believe that soap operas are "real," about how the actors who portray villains on these programs are often subjected to abusive mail from people who are convinced that these fictional creations are real personages. While that may not qualify as clinical madness, it is nonetheless delusional, and who among us would choose to be deluded if knowledge or education could save us?

So it's time for a little reality check. While it is true that literary and mythic figures often take on greater presence and force than do real personalities, it is important that the distinction be maintained. Many vibrant landscapes have been projected on our minds by writers, artists, and filmmakers, but we should be prepared to distinguish the painted landscape from terra firma, the imagined and dreamt terra incognita from the country next door.

We'll start with people. Real or imagined? Check it out.

TEST 2A
A TEST OF SANITY:
Fact or Fiction?

WHICH OF THE FOLLOWING PEOPLE ARE OR WERE REAL? WHICH ARE MAKE-BELIEVE? SINCE NOTHING RIDES ON THIS EXCEPT A SPURIOUS ASSESSMENT OF YOUR SANITY, DON'T GUESS. LUCKY TEST TAKERS, IN THE TIME-HONORED TRADITION OF MULTIPLE "GUESS" TESTS, COULD EASILY SCORE AROUND 50 PERCENT SIMPLY BY FLIPPING A COIN. YOU'LL HAVE TO DO BETTER THAN THAT TO BE JUDGED SANE BY THESE CRITERIA.

1. Learned Hand . . . . Fictional_____ Real_____
2. Jay Gatsby . . . . Fictional_____ Real_____
3. Steven Jobs. . . . . Fictional_____ Real_____
4. Belle Starr . . . . Fictional_____ Real_____
5. Uriah Heep . . . . Fictional_____ Real_____
6. Phileas Fogg. . . . . Fictional_____ Real_____
7. Engelbert Humperdinck . . . . Fictional_____ Real_____
8. Egbert Sousè . . . . Fictional_____ Real_____
9. Norton Simon . . . . Fictional_____ Real_____
10. Ed Norton . . . . Fictional_____ Real_____
11. Simon Legree . . . . Fictional_____ Real_____
12. Simon Bolivar . . . . Fictional_____ Real_____
13. T. Boone Pickens. . . . . Fictional_____ Real_____
14. Slim Pickens . . . . Fictional_____ Real_____
15. J. R. Ewing. . . . . Fictional_____ Real_____
16. J. Paul Getty . . . . Fictional_____ Real_____
17. J. C. Penney . . . . Fictional_____ Real_____
18. Vlad the Impaler . . . . Fictional_____ Real_____
19. Conan the Barbarian. . . . . Fictional_____ Real_____
20. The Birdman of Alcatraz . . . . Fictional_____ Real_____
21. The Incredible Shrinking Man . . . Fictional_____ Real_____
22. Harry Houdini . . . . Fictional_____ Real_____
23. The Elephant Man . . . . Fictional_____ Real_____
24. Zorba the Greek . . . . Fictional_____ Real_____
25. Jimmy the Greek . . . . Fictional_____ Real_____
26. El Greco. . . . . Fictional_____ Real_____
27. Thelonius Monk . . . . Fictional_____ Real_____
28. Humphry Clinker . . . . Fictional_____ Real_____
29. Humbert Humbert . . . . Fictional_____ Real_____
30. Herodotus . . . . Fictional_____ Real_____

31. Horatio Hornblower . . . . Fictional_____ Real_____
32. Abner Doubleday . . . . Fictional_____ Real_____
33. Mother Jones . . . . Fictional_____ Real_____
34. Mother Courage . . . . Fictional_____ Real_____
35. Grandma Moses . . . . Fictional_____ Real_____
36. Maria Tallchief . . . . Fictional_____ Real_____
37. Butterfly McQueen . . . . Fictional_____ Real_____
38. Typhoid Mary . . . . Fictional_____ Real_____
39. Calamity Jane . . . . Fictional_____ Real_____
40. Tugboat Annie . . . . Fictional_____ Real_____
41. Lizzie Borden . . . . Fictional_____ Real_____
42. Annie Oakley . . . . Fictional_____ Real_____
43. Carry Nation . . . . Fictional_____ Real_____
44. Tess of the d'Urbervilles . . . . Fictional_____ Real_____
45. Denmark Vesey . . . . Fictional_____ Real_____
46. Lawrence of Arabia . . . . Fictional_____ Real_____
47. Jack Armstrong . . . . Fictional_____ Real_____
48. Horatio Alger . . . . Fictional_____ Real_____
49. William Walker . . . . Fictional_____ Real_____
50. Luke Skywalker . . . . Fictional_____ Real_____
51. Nostradamus . . . . Fictional_____ Real_____
52. Nefertiti . . . . Fictional_____ Real_____
53. Madame Bovary . . . . Fictional_____ Real_____
54. Madame Tussaud . . . . Fictional_____ Real_____
55. The Earl of Sandwich . . . . Fictional_____ Real_____
56. The Earl of Greystoke . . . . Fictional_____ Real_____
57. Lady Macbeth . . . . Fictional_____ Real_____
58. Lady Di . . . . Fictional_____ Real_____
59. Madame Curie . . . . Fictional_____ Real_____
60. Virginia Dare . . . . Fictional_____ Real_____
61. Minnesota Fats . . . . Fictional_____ Real_____
62. Amarillo Slim . . . . Fictional_____ Real_____
63. Sergeant Preston . . . . Fictional_____ Real_____
64. Sergeant York . . . . Fictional_____ Real_____

65. Lieutenant William Calley....... Fictional_____ Real_____

66. Captain Ahab .... Fictional_____ Real_____

67. Corporal Klinger .... Fictional_____ Real_____

68. Uncle Remus................. Fictional_____ Real_____

69. Robert Strange McNamara....... Fictional_____ Real_____

70. Raskolnikov................. Fictional_____ Real_____

71. Rasputin .... Fictional_____ Real_____

72. Golda Meir .... Fictional_____ Real_____

73. Squeaky Fromme .... Fictional_____ Real_____

74. Ethan Frome .... Fictional_____ Real_____

75. Sir John Falstaff............. Fictional_____ Real_____

76. Sancho Panza .... Fictional_____ Real_____

77. Evel Kneivel .... Fictional_____ Real_____

78. Blanche Dubois.............. Fictional_____ Real_____

79. W. E. B. Du Bois .... Fictional_____ Real_____

80. Betty Boop................. Fictional_____ Real_____

81. Clara Bow .... Fictional_____ Real_____

82. Mr. Roberts .... Fictional_____ Real_____

83. Miniver Cheevy .... Fictional_____ Real_____

84. John Cheever............... Fictional_____ Real_____

85. King Wenceslas .... Fictional_____ Real_____

86. King Kamehameha .... Fictional_____ Real_____

87. Sydney Greenstreet .... Fictional_____ Real_____

88. Johnny Appleseed .... Fictional_____ Real_____

89. Amelia Earhart .... Fictional___ Real_____

90. Alger Hiss .... Fictional_____ Real_____

91. Ira Hayes .... Fictional_____ Real_____

92. Nat Turner................. Fictional_____ Real_____

93. Marquis de Sade .... Fictional_____ Real_____

94. Thomas Crapper............ Fictional_____ Real_____

95. Stonewall Jackson .... Fictional_____ Real_____

96. Natty Bumpo............... Fictional_____ Real_____

97. Cyrano de Bergerac.......... Fictional_____ Real_____

98. Ichabod Crane............... Fictional_____ Real_____

99. Rip Van Winkle. . . . . Fictional_____ Real_____

100. Robinson Crusoe. . . . . Fictional_____ Real_____

There, that's a hundred opportunities to distinguish between reality and imagination. How do you feel so far? You are probably either feeling very secure about your grip on reality—in which case you will want to press on to conquer new challenges—or you're feeling a little crazy and hope you might be able to reclaim some measure of sanity with additional questions.

While some fictional creations have a super-real presence, actual places are made of earth and air and water, are landscapes accessible to eyes and ears and nose, and can be located on maps. Most test takers, therefore, can only improve their hold on sanity by the following test.

Keep in mind that since opportunity is, after all, opportunity, each question opens to a landscape of additional things that you might learn and find fascinating, or that might prove enriching.

TEST 2B
THIS DOESN'T LOOK LIKE KANSAS:
Real Places, Imagined Locales

WHICH OF THE FOLLOWING PLACES ARE REAL, AND WHICH ARE MYTHICAL OR IMAGINED?

101. Katmandu . . . . Real_____ Imagined_____

102. Timbuktu . . . . Real_____ Imagined_____

103. Camelot . . . . Real_____ Imagined_____

104. Tasmania. . . . . Real_____ Imagined_____

105. Xanadu . . . . Real_____ Imagined_____

106. San Simeon. . . . . Real_____ Imagined_____

107. Lilliput . . . . Real_____ Imagined_____

108. Sri Lanka. . . . . Real_____ Imagined_____

109. Bali . . . . Real_____ Imagined_____

110. Erewhon . . . . Real_____ Imagined_____

111. Shangri-La. . . . . Real_____ Imagined_____

112. Boys Town. . . . . Real_____ Imagined_____

113. El Dorado . . . . Real_____ Imagined_____

114. Transylvania . . . . Real_____ Imagined_____

115. Peyton Place . . . . Real_____ Imagined_____

116. Atlantis	Real_____	Imagined_____
117. Sarawak	Real_____	Imagined_____
118. Fantasy Island	Real_____	Imagined_____
119. Skull Island	Real_____	Imagined_____
120. Yemen	Real_____	Imagined_____

You might have noticed that some of this "real or imagined" business is not quite so cut-and-dried as it might first appear. If it struck you that way, then you might be one of those people who are too smart to do well on tests. You start asking yourself philosophical questions about the nature of "the real." You equivocate, carry on an internal dialogue, begin to get ideas about things (because, after all, knowledge begets ideas). If this were a scholastic test, all that time thinking and equivocating would work against you. Time would be running and you would likely find yourself with a lot of unanswered questions when the test proctor called the tests in. Testing, as far as schools are concerned, honors quick responses. Thinking too much is inimical to that process.

But let's say you're still not sure you've got a firm grip on reality. Let's say you've checked the answers, scored yourself, and find that you've only got 68 percent correct so far. That's probably in the "sane" range, but not too far into it. If you're still seeking assurances that you are in touch with reality, try these additional questions about pairs of people. The thing with pairs is, you've got two people to think about. If you know that one of them is real, you can be pretty sure that the partner is real, too. Try it. You've got little to lose—except your sanity.

TEST 2C
ME AND MY SHADOW:
Real or Imagined Teams, Pairs, or Couples

WHICH OF THE FOLLOWING PAIRED NAMES ARE (OR WERE) REAL, AND WHICH WERE FICTIONAL OR IMAGINED?

121. Chan and Eng	Real_____	Imagined_____
122. Cheech and Chong	Real_____	Imagined_____
123. Burns and Allen	Real_____	Imagined_____
124. Heloise and Abelard	Real_____	Imagined_____
125. Siskel and Ebert	Real_____	Imagined_____
126. Leopold and Loeb	Real_____	Imagined_____
127. Quasimodo and Esmeralda	Real_____	Imagined_____

128. Stanley and Livingstone........ Real_____ Imagined_____

129. Currier and Ives.............. Real_____ Imagined_____

130. Pyramus and Thisbe .... Real_____ Imagined_____

131. Puss and Boots.............. Real_____ Imagined_____

132. Daphnis and Chloe .... Real_____ Imagined_____

133. Rosencrantz and Guildenstern .. Real_____ Imagined_____

134. Antony and Cleopatra .... Real_____ Imagined_____

135. Robin Hood and Maid Marian... Real_____ Imagined_____

It might seem more than a little presumptuous to set up these tests as a measure of anyone's sanity. Even though this notion is offered facetiously, and even though no one would measure sanity by a test of knowledge, think of all the determinations that *are* made on the basis of testing. Very early on in our educations the schools have usually sorted us out, proclaimed that some of us are slow and some quick, some dull and some bright. There is always, in those godlike judgments, the element of self-fulfilling prophecy. As a community college teacher, I've seen thousands of people who bear the scars of these often capricious assessments.

There are, of course, individual differences in intelligence or learning ability, but the obsession with testing and categorizing people often stands in the way of the very learning it is supposed to facilitate. The medical profession has as its primary commandment the imprecation "First, do no harm." The profession of teaching does, I think, incalculable harm—harm to the students and to the purpose of education. If the medical profession put the disproportionate percentage of effort into diagnosis that the teaching profession puts into testing, our mortality rate would soar. We would surely not be concerned about overpopulation, especially if, as so often happens in education, treatment slackened after the diagnosis was made.

But you're still in the midst of taking your own measure, not yet finished with the task of assessing your grip on reality. This last leg of the reality check is mercifully brief, but it provides an opportunity to rack up more points.

TEST 2D
GROUP IDENTITY

BEFORE JOINING A GROUP, IT MIGHT BE USEFUL TO KNOW IF THE GROUP IS REAL. WHICH OF THESE ARE (OR WERE) REAL AND WHICH AREN'T (OR WEREN'T)?

136. The Houyhnhnms .... Real____ Fictional____

137. Mugwumps .... Real____ Fictional____

138. Carpetbaggers .... Real____ Fictional____

139. Tralfamadorians .... Real____ Fictional____

140. Wobblies .... Real____ Fictional____

141. Munchkins .... Real____ Fictional____

142. Zouaves .... Real____ Fictional____

143. Flatheads .... Real____ Fictional____

144. Roundheads .... Real____ Fictional____

145. The Knownothings .... Real____ Fictional____

146. The Three Musketeers .... Real____ Fictional____

147. The Wild Bunch .... Real____ Fictional____

148. The Rough Riders .... Real____ Fictional____

149. The Jayhawkers .... Real____ Fictional____

150. Zoroastrians .... Real____ Fictional____

So that's done. If your test results indicate that you haven't performed as well as you thought you would, then you can take some comfort in the idea that in the late twentieth century we are all a little crazy. You can also take comfort in the idea that this measure of sanity (or lack of same) will require no expensive therapy, no dreary trips to psychoanalysts. All you have to do is continue to acquire knowledge so that your grip on reality grows less slippery.

TEST 2A ANSWERS

1. Learned Hand (1872–1961)—*Real* American jurist

2. Jay Gatsby—*Fictional* main character in *The Great Gatsby* (1925) by American novelist F. Scott Fitzgerald

3. Steven Jobs (1955–)—*Real* American entrepeneur and electronics engineer; co-founder of Apple Computers, Inc., with Stephen Wozniak

4. Belle Starr (1848–1889)—*Real* nineteenth-century American outlaw

5. Uriah Heep—*Fictional* character in *David Copperfield* (1849–1850) by English novelist Charles Dickens

6. Phileas Fogg—*Fictional* character in *Around the World in Eighty Days* (1873) by French writer Jules Verne

7. Engelbert Humperdinck (1854–1921)—*Real* German composer

8. Egbert Sousè—*Fictional* character/pseudonym created by American actor/humorist W. C. Fields

9. Norton Simon (1907–)—*Real* twentieth century American businessman

10. Ed Norton—*Fictional* character played by Art Carney in the "Honeymooners" segment of *The Jackie Gleason Show*

11. Simon Legree—*Fictional* character in *Uncle Tom's Cabin* (1851–1852) by American author Harriet Beecher Stowe

12. Simon Bolivar (1783–1830)—*Real* South American general. Hero of South American fight for independence from Spain

13. T. Boone Pickens (1928–)—*Real* twentieth-century American businessman

14. Slim Pickens (1919–1983)—*Real* American rodeo clown and cowboy actor Louis Bert Lindley, Jr.

15. J. R. Ewing—*Fictional* character on the *Dallas* TV series, played by Larry Hagman

16. J. Paul Getty (1892–1976)—*Real* American businessman. Was one of the richest men in the world

17. J. C. Penney—*Real* James Cash Penney (1875–1971), U.S. businessman. Founder of J. C. Penney Company, which became the second largest nonfood retailer in the United States

18. Vlad the Impaler—*Real* Vlad Tepes (1432?–1477), an Eastern European folk hero who became the inspiration for the novel *Dracula* (1897) by Irish novelist Bram Stoker

19. Conan the Barbarian—*Fictional* film character played by Arnold Schwarzenegger, based on a character created by Robert E. Howard

20. The Birdman of Alcatraz—*Real* Robert Stroud (1890–1963), a convicted murderer whose life was the basis for the

movie *The Birdman of Alcatraz* (1962), which starred Burt Lancaster

21. The Incredible Shrinking Man—*Fictional* character played by Grant Williams in the movie of the same name (1957) written by Richard Matheson

22. Harry Houdini—*Real* Ehrich Weiss (1874–1926), an escape artist and magician of Hungarian descent

23. The Elephant Man—*Real* John Merrick (1863–1890), whose tragic life was the subject of the movie *The Elephant Man*, with John Hurt in the title role

24. Zorba the Greek—*Fictional* movie (1964) character played by Anthony Quinn, based on a novel of the same name by Nikos Kazantzakis

25. Jimmy the Greek—*Real* Dimitrios Synodinos, Las Vegas oddsmaker and gambler

26. El Greco—*Real* Domenicos Theotocopoulos (ca. 1541–1614), Spanish painter of Greek origin

27. Thelonius Monk (1920–1982)—*Real* twentieth-century American jazz pianist

28. Humphry Clinker—*Fictional* novel (1771) by Scottish writer Tobias Smollet

29. Humbert Humbert—*Fictional* character in the novel *Lolita* (1955) by Russian/American novelist Vladimir Nabokov

30. Herodotus (484?–425? B.C.)—*Real* Greek historian, the "Father of History"

31. Horatio Hornblower—*Fictional* main character in stories of the Royal Navy by English author C. S. Forester (1899–1966) (Forester also wrote *The African Queen*.)

32. Abner Doubleday (1819–1893)—*Real* Union general in the U.S. Civil War. Once thought to have been the inventor of baseball

33. Mother Jones—*Real* Mary Harris (1830–1930), active in the U.S. labor movement

34. Mother Courage—*Fictional* character in the play *Mother Courage and her Children* (1941) by German dramatist Bertolt Brecht

35. Grandma Moses—*Real* Anna Mary Robertson Moses (1860–1961), American artist known for her primitive paintings depicting scenes of rural life

36. Maria Tallchief (1925–)—*Real* American ballerina of Osage Indian descent

37. Butterfly McQueen—*Real* American actress. Played Prissy, a supporting role in *Gone With the Wind* (1939)

38. Typhoid Mary—*Real* Mary Mallon (1870?–1938), a New York cook who was a typhoid carrier

39. Calamity Jane— *Real* Martha Jane Burke (1852–1903), American frontier figure

40. Tugboat Annie—*Fictional* title of an American movie (1933) with Marie Dressler and Wallace Beery

41. Lizzie Borden (1860–1927)—*Real* American woman accused of the ax murders of her father and stepmother. She was acquitted and the case remains unsolved

42. Annie Oakley—*Real* Phoebe Anne Oakley Moses (1860–1926). Expert markswoman and performer in Buffalo Bill Cody's Wild West Show

43. Carry Nation (1846–1911)—*Real* U.S. temperance advocate. Influential in passage of the eighteenth amendment to the Constitution

44. Tess of the d'Urbervilles—*Fictional* heroine of an 1891 novel of the same name by English author Thomas Hardy

45. Denmark Vesey (1767–1822)—*Real* American black who led a slave rebellion in 1822 for which he was hanged

46. Lawrence of Arabia—*Real* T. E. Lawrence (1888–1935), British adventurer. His book, *The Seven Pillars of Wisdom*, chronicles his adventures in Arabia. Died in a motorcycle accident

47. Jack Armstrong—*Fictional* lead character in the popular radio show *Jack Armstrong, the All-American Boy*, first broadcast in 1933

48. Horatio Alger (1832–1899)—*Real* Unitarian minister who wrote rags-to-riches stories for boys

49. William Walker (1824–1860)—*Real* nineteenth-century American adventurer. Declared himself president of Nicaragua in 1856

50. Luke Skywalker—*Fictional* hero in the space fantasy movie *Star Wars* (1977), written and directed by George Lucas

51. Nostradamus—*Real* Michel de Nostredame (1503–1566), French astrologer and physician

52. Nefertiti—*Real* fourteenth-century B.C. Egyptian queen noted for her beauty

53. Madame Bovary—*Fictional* heroine of a novel (1857) of same name by French writer Gustave Flaubert

54. Madame Tussaud—*Real* Marie Gresholtz (1760–1850). Operated a wax museum in London in the early nineteenth century

55. The Earl of Sandwich—*Real* John Montague (1718–1792), an English nobleman who is thought to have invented the sandwich

56. The Earl of Greystoke—*Fictional* character, also known as Tarzan, created (1914) by American writer Edgar Rice Burroughs

57. Lady Macbeth—*Fictional* character in the play *Macbeth* (ca. 1605) by William Shakespeare

58. Lady Di—*Real* Lady Diana Spencer (1961–), who became the Princess of Wales when she married England's Prince Charles on July 29, 1981

59. Madame Curie—*Real* Manya Sklodowska, also known as Marie Curie (1867–1934), Polish-born French chemist. Recipient of two Nobel prizes for science

60. Virginia Dare (1587–?)—*Real* first English child born in America

61. Minnesota Fats—*Real* Rudolf Wanderone, Jr., American pool player. Jackie Gleason played a character by this name in the movie *The Hustler* (1961)

62. Amarillo Slim—*Real* Thomas Austin Preston, Jr., contemporary American poker player

63. Sergeant Preston—*Fictional* lead character in the radio show *Challenge of the Yukon*, first broadcast in 1947

64. Sergeant York—*Real* Alvin Cullum York (1887–1964), American hero of World War I

65. Lieutenant William Calley—*Real* U.S. Army officer in charge during the My Lai incident (1968) during the Vietnam War

66. Captain Ahab—*Fictional* character in *Moby-Dick* (1851) by American novelist Herman Melville

67. Corporal Klinger—*Fictional* character in the movie *M*A*S*H* (1970) and in the TV series of the same name

68. Uncle Remus—*Fictional* character in the book *Uncle Remus, His Songs and Sayings* by American writer Joel Chandler Harris, and in a Walt Disney movie *Song of the South* (1946)

69. Robert Strange McNamara (1916–)—*Real* former president of Ford Motor Company, he served as the Secretary of Defense under Presidents John Kennedy and Lyndon Johnson

70. Raskolnikov—*Fictional* character in the novel *Crime and Punishment* (1866) by Russian writer Fyodor Dostoyevsky

71. Rasputin—*Real* Grigori Yefimovich (1872–1916), Russian faith healer and advisor to Czar Nicholas II and Czarina Alexandra Feodorovna

72. Golda Meir—*Real* Goldie Mabovitch (1898–1978), prime minister of Israel, 1969–1974

73. Squeaky Fromme—*Real* Lynette Alice Fromme (ca. 1949–), member of the infamous Manson family

74. Ethan Frome—*Fictional* character in the novel of the same name (1911) by American writer Edith Wharton

75. Sir John Falstaff—*Fictional* character in *King Henry IV*, parts 1 and 2 (ca. 1597) by William Shakespeare

76. Sancho Panza—*Fictional* sidekick of Don Quixote in the novel *Don Quixote* (1605–1615) by Spanish novelist Miguel de Cervantes Saavedra

77. Evel Kneivel—*Real* twentieth-century American daredevil

78. Blanche Dubois—*Fictional* character in the play *A Streetcar Named Desire* (1947) by American author Tennessee Williams. Vivien Leigh played this part in the movie version (1951)

79. W. E. B. Du Bois (1868–1963)—*Real* American educator, writer, and civil rights leader who cofounded the National Association for the Advancement of Colored People (NAACP) in 1909–1910

80. Betty Boop—*Fictional* cartoon character created by Max Fleischer

81. Clara Bow (1905–1965)—*Real* American movie actress. Known as the "It Girl" as a result of her appearance in the movie *It* in 1927

82. Mr. Roberts—*Fictional* title character in the novel *Mister Roberts* by Thomas Heggen and the play (ca. 1947–1948) by Thomas Heggen and Joshua Logan. Henry Fonda played the role in the movie version (1955)

83. Miniver Cheevy—*Fictional* character in a poem by American poet Edwin Arlington Robinson that appeared in *The Town Down the River* (1910)

84. John Cheever (1912–1982)—*Real* Pulitzer Prize–winning American writer

85. King Wenceslas (1361–1419)—*Real* king of Germany and Holy Roman emperor. Also served as king of Bohemia (1378–1419) as Wenceslas IV

86. King Kamehameha (ca. 1758–1819)—*Real* Hawaiian king/ruler

87. Sydney Greenstreet (1879–1954)—*Real* British actor who made his film debut in *The Maltese Falcon* (1941)

88. Johnny Appleseed—*Real* John Chapman (1774–1845), legendary American pioneer

89. Amelia Earhart (1897–1937?)—*Real* pioneering American aviatrix who disappeared during a flight around the world in 1937

90. Alger Hiss (1904–)—*Real* U.S. public official convicted of perjury in 1950 during the red-baiting scare of that time

91. Ira Hayes (1923–1955)—*Real* Pima Indian hero of World War II. Was one of the six soldiers who raised the American flag on Iwo Jima after the defeat of the Japanese in 1945

92. Nat Turner (1800–1831)—*Real* American slave who led a slave rebellion in 1831. Subject of the Pulitzer Prize–winning book, *The Confessions of Nat Turner* by William Styron (1967)

93. Marquis de Sade—*Real* Donatien Alphonse Francois Comte de Sade (1740–1814), French author. The word *sadism* is derived from his name

94. Thomas Crapper—*Real* nineteenth-century English inventor sometimes credited with the invention of the flush toilet (1882)

95. Stonewall Jackson—*Real* Thomas Jonathan Jackson (1824–

1863), Confederate general during the American Civil War. Accidentally killed by his own men.

96. Natty Bumpo—*Fictional* character in the Leatherstocking tales, a series of novels by American author James Fenimore Cooper (1789–1851) modeled on American frontiersman Daniel Boone

97. Cyrano de Bergerac (1619–1655)—*Real* French poet and novelist known for his huge nose. Subject of a drama (1897) of the same name written by French author Edmond Rostand

98. Ichabod Crane—*Fictional* character in the story *The Legend of Sleepy Hollow* (1820) by American writer Washington Irving

99. Rip Van Winkle—*Fictional* title character of a story (1819) that appeared with Ichabod Crane in *The Sketch Book* by Washington Irving. Irving used the pseudonymn Geoffrey Crayon when he wrote these pieces.

100. Robinson Crusoe—*Fictional* title character of a novel (1719) by English writer Daniel Defoe

TEST 2B ANSWERS

101. Katmandu—*Real* capitol of Nepal

102. Timbuktu—*Real* town in central Mali

103. Camelot—*Imagined* legendary English town of King Arthur and the Knights of the Round Table

104. Tasmania—*Real* island south of Australia

105. Xanadu—*Imagined* location in the poem *Kubla Khan* (published 1816) by English poet Samuel Taylor Coleridge

106. San Simeon—*Real* location on the Pacific coast in California of the Hearst castle

107. Lilliput—*Imagined* land of the Little People in *Gulliver's Travels* (1726) by English writer Jonathan Swift

108. Sri Lanka—*Real* official name of Ceylon, an island off the southeast tip of India

109. Bali—*Real* Indonesian island

110. Erewhon—*Imagined* title of a book (1872) by English author Samuel Butler. Erewhon is an anagram for "nowhere"

111. Shangri-La—*Imagined* idyllic location of the novel *Lost Horizon* (1933) by English author James Hilton

112. Boys Town—*Real* town near Omaha, Nebraska, founded in 1917 by Father Flanagan, a Roman Catholic priest, as a shelter for homeless boys

113. El Dorado—*Imagined* place, originally of Spanish legend, supposed to be rich in gold

114. Transylvania—*Real* region in Romania

115. Peyton Place—*Imagined* location of the novel (1956) of the same name by American writer Grace Metalious

116. Atlantis—*Imagined* island of Greek legend that was supposed to have sunk into the ocean. Some scholars think it may have existed

117. Sarawak—*Real* Malaysian state in Borneo

118. Fantasy Island—*Imagined* location of a successful television show of the same name first broadcast in 1978

119. Skull Island—*Imagined* legendary birthplace of King Kong

120. Yemen—*Real* Arabian country located on the Red Sea

TEST 2C ANSWERS

121. Chang and Eng (1811–1874)—*Real* original Siamese twins born in Meklong, Siam. They immigrated to America and became naturalized citizens. They traveled in the United States and Great Britain as an exhibition.

122. Cheech and Chong—*Real* American comedy team of the 1970s and 1980s

123. Burns and Allen—*Real* George Burns and Gracie Allen, husband and wife comedy team of American radio and television

124. Heloise and Abelard—*Real* tragic eleventh-century French lovers

125. Siskel and Ebert—*Real* Gene Siskel and Roger Ebert, multimedia contemporary American film critics

126. Leopold and Loeb—*Real* infamous kidnappers and murderers, Nathan Leopold, Jr. (1904–1971), and Richard A. Loeb (1905–1931). Tried to commit the "perfect crime," but didn't succeed.

127. Quasimodo and Esmeralda—*Imagined*. Quasimodo is the main character in the novel *The Hunchback of Notre Dame* (1831) by French writer Victor Hugo. Esmeralda is the gypsy girl he loves.

128. Stanley and Livingstone—*Real* Sir Henry Morton Stanley (1841–1904), British explorer and journalist, and David Livingstone (1813–1873), a Scottish explorer. Stanley found

Livingstone in 1871 in Africa, where Livingstone was searching for the source of the Nile River

129. Currier and Ives—*Real* Nathaniel Currier (1813–1888) and James Ives (1824–1895), partners in a New York firm that produced popular prints of nineteenth-century American life

130. Pyramus and Thisbe—*Imagined* lovers in the classical myth whose story appears in the fourth book of Ovid's *Metamorphoses*

131. Puss and Boots—*Imagined* children's nursery rhyme

132. Daphnis and Chloe—*Imagined* hero and heroine of the bucolic romance (ca. second or third century A.D.) of the same name by Greek writer Longus

133. Rosencrantz and Guildenstern—*Imagined* courtiers in Shakespeare's *Hamlet*

134. Antony and Cleopatra—*Real* Marc Antony, a Roman politician who married Cleopatra, Queen of Egypt, in 36 B.C.

135. Robin Hood and Maid Marian—*Imagined* lovers of twelfth-century English legend

TEST 2D ANSWERS

136. The Houyhnhnms—*Fictional* term coined by Jonathan Swift in *Gulliver's Travels* designating a race of horses with human powers

137. Mugwumps—*Real* members of the Republican party who did not support the party ticket in the 1884 elections in which Grover Cleveland defeated James Blaine for president

138. Carpetbaggers—*Real* northerners who moved south following the Civil War hoping to profit from the unstable conditions there

139. Tralfamadorians—*Fictional* extraterrestrial beings created by American author Kurt Vonnegut in his novel *Slaughterhouse Five* (1969)

140. Wobblies—*Real.* This name was given to Industrial Workers of the World (IWW) union organized in Chicago in 1905

141. Munchkins—*Fictional.* This term was coined by American author L. Frank Baum in *The Wizard of Oz* to designate small, imaginary beings

142. Zouaves—*Real.* A tribe in Algeria; also a French infantry

unit or American Civil War units that adopted variations of Zouave clothing

143. Flatheads—*Real* North American Indians of western Montana, also known as the Salish Indians

144. Roundheads—*Real* members of the Puritan or Parlimentary party during the English civil war (1642–1652)

145. The Knownothings—*Real* members of a secret political party in the United States during the 1850s. Members claimed ignorance of the party's activities, hence the name.

146. The Three Musketeers—*Fictional* characters in an 1844 novel of the same name by French author Alexandre Dumas

147. The Wild Bunch—*Real* outlaw band headed by Butch Cassidy in the 1890s

148. The Rough Riders—*Real* volunteer U.S. cavalry regiment organized for service in the Spanish-American War (1898) by Theodore Roosevelt and Leonard Wood

149. The Jayhawkers—*Real* abolitionists in Kansas and Missouri during the U.S. Civil War

150. Zoroastrians—*Real* followers of Zoroaster, a religious leader in Persia prior to the introduction of Islam in that country in the seventh century

SCORING

There are 150 questions in this chapter. In order to qualify as one who is in touch with reality, you should have gotten a score of at least 100 questions correct. For a more precise and clinical diagnosis of your sanity, consult the following mechanism:

> 101–150: Count yourself among the sane.
> 76–100: Mildly delusional.
> 51–75: Wildly delusional.
> 50 or less: Living in a world of your own.

CHAPTER THREE

GENDER CONFUSION AND OTHER MYSTERIES

There are three sections to the test in this chapter. Each is meant to challenge your powers of discrimination. Although the word *discrimination* has acquired a host of legitimately negative connotations, the word also defines a quite positive human skill. In fact, education gives us the ability to make ever more refined discriminations—between phylum and order in taxonomy, between romantic and baroque in music, between Elizabethan and Augustan in British history. As we progress through education and through life, our ability to make discriminations is one of the marks of our growth in intelligence and experience. A baby may not be able to discriminate between hot and cold or pointed and blunt, but learns those lessons soon enough, and so gains discriminatory ability. Our progress after that is largely measured by how many discriminations we can make, and how fine those discriminations are. The IQ test and the Scholastic Aptitude Test (SAT, the bane of every high school kid) are both largely based on testing the ability to make discriminations.

The first part of this chapter's test gives you the opportunity to make discriminations between men and women. During the 1960s, when long hair on males was considered a threatening deviation from the accepted codes of appearance, it was common to hear the complaint that it was hard to tell if a long-haired person was a boy or a girl. I always wondered at the poor powers of discrimination reflected in that complaint, since I think the physical differences between men and women are easy to see. However, with only a name as a clue, those of you who feel perfectly confident in your ability to make the elementary discrimination between male and female may find it harder than you think. This test is meant to challenge that confidence. Though this book is meant to inspire the confidence that encourages further learning, overconfidence can lead to complacency and deserves to be shaken just a bit.

It might interest you, considering the subject of the following questions, to know that the word *test* is related to the word *testicles*. *Testis*, from which both words derive, literally means "cup." More specifically, it is thought to have originated from the old French word for the sort of cup used by alchemists to separate gold from baser metals. Metaphorically, then, the word *test* has to do with sorting out the precious from the lesser ore. This bit of knowledge—seen by some as pedantic or trivial— encourages another way of thinking about the process, aims, and assumptions of testing.

At any rate, you can do well on this first test. We have a great deal of experience with discrimination, in both positive and negative senses of the word, and we can tell the difference between men and women, can't we?

TEST 3A
GENDER CONFUSION

ARE THE FOLLOWING PEOPLE MALE OR FEMALE? YOU'VE GOT A FIFTY-FIFTY CHANCE ON THIS ONE, BUT I'D ADVISE AGAINST GUESSING. A MISTAKE OF THIS KIND CAN HAVE EMBARRASSING CONSEQUENCES.

1. George Sand .... Male_____ Female_____

2. Flannery O'Connor.............. Male_____ Female_____

3. Evelyn Waugh .... Male_____ Female_____

4. Hecuba....................... Male_____ Female_____

5. Isak Dinesen .... Male_____ Female_____

6. Marion Morrison .... Male_____ Female_____

7. E. B. White .... Male_____ Female_____

8. Babe Didrikson................. Male_____ Female_____

9. Camille Saint-Saëns .... Male_____ Female_____

10. Sappho....................... Male_____ Female_____

11. Yo-Yo Ma .... Male_____ Female_____

12. Reza Pahlevi .... Male_____ Female_____

13. Ovid........................ Male_____ Female_____

14. Vidkun Quisling............... Male_____ Female_____

15. Carson McCullers.............. Male_____ Female_____

16. Osceola . . . . Male_____ Female_____
17. George Eliot . . . . Male_____ Female_____
18. A. A. Milne . . . . Male_____ Female_____
19. Stevie Smith . . . . Male_____ Female_____
20. Rainer Maria Rilke . . . . Male_____ Female_____
21. Francis Marion . . . . Male_____ Female_____
22. Yasuhiro Nakasone . . . . Male_____ Female_____
23. Sun Yat-sen . . . . Male_____ Female_____
24. Glenn Close . . . . Male_____ Female_____
25. Vachel Lindsay . . . . Male_____ Female_____
26. Kobo Abe . . . . Male_____ Female_____
27. Sacajawea . . . . Male_____ Female_____
28. Osiris . . . . Male_____ Female_____
29. Ellery Queen . . . . Male_____ Female_____
30. Alice Cooper . . . . Male_____ Female_____
31. Fra Filippo Lippi . . . . Male_____ Female_____
32. Toshiro Mifune . . . . Male_____ Female_____
33. Flo Ziegfeld . . . . Male_____ Female_____
34. The Valkyries . . . . Male_____ Female_____
35. Joan Miro . . . . Male_____ Female_____
36. Pygmalion . . . . Male_____ Female_____
37. Piaf . . . . Male_____ Female_____
38. Narcissus . . . . Male_____ Female_____
39. Tecumseh . . . . Male_____ Female_____
40. Pol Pot . . . . Male_____ Female_____
41. Saint Frances Xavier Cabrini . . . . . . Male_____ Female_____
42. Somerset Maugham . . . . Male_____ Female_____
43. Amedeo Modigliani . . . . Male_____ Female_____
44. Jean LaFitte . . . . Male_____ Female_____
45. Jeane Duane Jordon Kirkpatrick . . . Male_____ Female_____
46. Basho . . . . Male_____ Female_____
47. Sandy Koufax . . . . Male_____ Female_____
48. Liliuokalani . . . . Male_____ Female_____
49. Ceres . . . . Male_____ Female_____

50. Joyce Kilmer . . . . Male____ Female____
51. W. C. Handy . . . . Male____ Female____
52. Chiang Kai-shek . . . . Male____ Female____
53. Odin. . . . . Male____ Female____
54. Aesop. Male____ Female____
55. Svetlana Alliluyeva. . . . . Male____ Female____
56. The Furies . . . . Male____ Female____
57. Nebuchadnezzar . . . . Male____ Female____
58. Shiva . . . . Male____ Female____
59. E. Power Biggs . . . . Male____ Female____
60. Valéry Giscard d'Estaing . . . . Male____ Female____
61. Countee Cullen. . . . . Male____ Female____
62. Hammurabi. . . . . Male____ Female____
63. Fran Tarkenton . . . . Male____ Female____
64. Sun Myung Moon. . . . . Male____ Female____
65. Imamu Amiri Baraka . . . . Male____ Female____
66. Molech. . . . . Male____ Female____
67. B. F. Skinner . . . . Male____ Female____
68. Khalil Gibran . . . . Male____ Female____
69. Saladin. . . . . Male____ Female____
70. Circe . . . . Male____ Female____
71. Hideki Tojo . . . . Male____ Female____
72. Sirhan Sirhan . . . . Male____ Female____
73. Corazon Aquino . . . . Male____ Female____
74. Yukio Mishima. . . . . Male____ Female____
75. Benazir Bhutto . . . . Male____ Female____

From distinguishing gender, we'll turn to distinguishing function. It begins with the word, with the naming of things. To know a thing is to know its name. In creation stories from every culture, the word figures importantly as the instrument human beings employ to make the world comprehensible.

We think with words; words give structure to our inchoate feelings. It is not an exaggeration to say that unless there is a word for a thing, that thing does not exist for us. Whenever a new thing is discovered, the first way of dealing with it is to give it a name.

The following section challenges your command of the names of things. Some are common, some are obscure. You need not define each word; you need only use your common knowledge to determine what you do with each item listed.

TEST 3B
FUNCTIONAL KNOWLEDGE

WHAT IS THE PROPER USE OF THE FOLLOWING THINGS? PUT A CHECK MARK NEXT TO THE APPROPRIATE CHOICE.

76. Plaice . . . . Wear It____ Eat It____ Read It____
    Spend It____ Drive It____ Fly It____
    Drink It____

77. Lorgnette . . . . Wear It____ Eat It____ Read It____
    Spend It____ Drive It____ Fly It____
    Drink It____

78. Snood . . . . Wear It____ Eat It____ Read It____
    Spend It____ Drive It____ Fly It____
    Drink It____

79. Ouzo . . . . Wear It____ Eat It____ Read It____
    Spend It____ Drive It____ Fly It____
    Drink It____

80. Dashiki . . . . Wear It____ Eat It____ Read It____
    Spend It____ Drive It____ Fly It____
    Drink It____

81. Pfennig . . . . Wear It____ Eat It____ Read It____
    Spend It____ Drive It____ Fly It____
    Drink It____

82. Codpiece . . . . Wear It____ Eat It____ Read It____
    Spend It____ Drive It____ Fly It____
    Drink It____

83. Fernet Branca . . . . . . Wear It____ Eat It____ Read It____
    Spend It____ Drive It____ Fly It____
    Drink It____

84. Sopwith Camel . . . . Wear It____ Eat It____ Read It____
    Spend It____ Drive It____ Fly It____
    Drink It____

85. Villanelle . . . . Wear It_____ Eat It_____ Read It_____
Spend It_____ Drive It_____ Fly It_____
Drink It_____

86. Farthing . . . . Wear It_____ Eat It_____ Read It_____
Spend It_____ Drive It_____ Fly It_____
Drink It_____

87. Burnoose. . . . . Wear It_____ Eat It_____ Read It_____
Spend It_____ Drive It_____ Fly It_____
Drink It_____

88. Gherkin . . . . Wear It_____ Eat It_____ Read It_____
Spend It_____ Drive It_____ Fly It_____
Drink It_____

89. Mantilla . . . . Wear It_____ Eat It_____ Read It_____
Spend It_____ Drive It_____ Fly It_____
Drink It_____

90. Jerkin . . . . Wear It_____ Eat It_____ Read It_____
Spend It_____ Drive It_____ Fly It_____
Drink It_____

91. Stuka. . . . . Wear It_____ Eat It_____ Read It_____
Spend It_____ Drive It_____ Fly It_____
Drink It_____

92. Shoat. . . . . Wear It_____ Eat It_____ Read It_____
Spend It_____ Drive It_____ Fly It_____
Drink It_____

93. Slivovitz . . . . Wear It_____ Eat It_____ Read It_____
Spend It_____ Drive It_____ Fly It_____
Drink It_____

94. Stutz-Bearcat . . . . . . Wear It_____ Eat It_____ Read It_____
Spend It_____ Drive It_____ Fly It_____
Drink It_____

95. Potboiler . . . . Wear It_____ Eat It_____ Read It_____
Spend It_____ Drive It_____ Fly It_____
Drink It_____

96. Rondelet . . . . Wear It_____ Eat It_____ Read It_____
Spend It_____ Drive It_____ Fly It_____
Drink It_____

97. Furbelow . . . . Wear It____ Eat It____ Read It____
 Spend It____ Drive It____ Fly It____
 Drink It____

98. Dhoti . . . . Wear It____ Eat It____ Read It____
 Spend It____ Drive It____ Fly It____
 Drink It____

99. Chorizo . . . . Wear It____ Eat It____ Read It____
 Spend It____ Drive It____ Fly It____
 Drink It____

100. Chaddar . . . . Wear It____ Eat It____ Read It____
 Spend It____ Drive It____ Fly It____
 Drink It____

101. Dry Sack . . . . Wear It____ Eat It____ Read It____
 Spend It____ Drive It____ Fly It____
 Drink It____

102. Bodice Ripper . . . . . Wear It____ Eat It____ Read It____
 Spend It____ Drive It____ Fly It____
 Drink It____

103. Spruce Goose . . . . . Wear It____ Eat It____ Read It____
 Spend It____ Drive It____ Fly It____
 Drink It____

104. Miter . . . . Wear It____ Eat It____ Read It____
 Spend It____ Drive It____ Fly It____
 Drink It____

105. Montrachet . . . . Wear It____ Eat It____ Read It____
 Spend It____ Drive It____ Fly It____
 Drink It____

106. Finnan Haddie . . . . Wear It____ Eat It____ Read It____
 Spend It____ Drive It____ Fly It____
 Drink It____

107. Farinaceous . . . . Wear It____ Eat It____ Read It____
 Spend It____ Drive It____ Fly It____
 Drink It____

108. Babushka . . . . Wear It____ Eat It____ Read It____
 Spend It____ Drive It____ Fly It____
 Drink It____

109. Grignolino . . . . Wear It_____ Eat It_____ Read It_____
Spend It_____ Drive It_____ Fly It_____
Drink It_____

110. Stilton . . . . Wear It_____ Eat It_____ Read It_____
Spend It_____ Drive It_____ Fly It_____
Drink It_____

111. Bolero . . . . Wear It_____ Eat It_____ Read It_____
Spend It_____ Drive It_____ Fly It_____
Drink It_____

112. Cous-cous . . . . Wear It_____ Eat It_____ Read It_____
Spend It_____ Drive It_____ Fly It_____
Drink It_____

113. Kirtle . . . . Wear It_____ Eat It_____ Read It_____
Spend It_____ Drive It_____ Fly It_____
Drink It_____

114. Krona . . . . Wear It_____ Eat It_____ Read It_____
Spend It_____ Drive It_____ Fly It_____
Drink It_____

115. Pince-nez . . . . Wear It_____ Eat It_____ Read It_____
Spend It_____ Drive It_____ Fly It_____
Drink It_____

116. Roman à clef . . . . . Wear It_____ Eat It_____ Read It_____
Spend It_____ Drive It_____ Fly It_____
Drink It_____

117. Ort . . . . Wear It_____ Eat It_____ Read It_____
Spend It_____ Drive It_____ Fly It_____
Drink It_____

118. Bel Paese . . . . Wear It_____ Eat It_____ Read It_____
Spend It_____ Drive It_____ Fly It_____
Drink It_____

119. Haiku . . . . Wear It_____ Eat It_____ Read It_____
Spend It_____ Drive It_____ Fly It_____
Drink It_____

120. Caftan . . . . Wear It_____ Eat It_____ Read It_____
Spend It_____ Drive It_____ Fly It_____
Drink It_____

121. Lira . . . . Wear It____ Eat It____ Read It____ Spend It____ Drive It____ Fly It____ Drink It____

122. Novella . . . . Wear It____ Eat It____ Read It____ Spend It____ Drive It____ Fly It____ Drink It____

123. Redingote . . . . Wear It____ Eat It____ Read It____ Spend It____ Drive It____ Fly It____ Drink It____

124. Retsina . . . . Wear It____ Eat It____ Read It____ Spend It____ Drive It____ Fly It____ Drink It____

125. Spad . . . . Wear It____ Eat It____ Read It____ Spend It____ Drive It____ Fly It____ Drink It____

126. Karmann Ghia . . . . Wear It____ Eat It____ Read It____ Spend It____ Drive It____ Fly It____ Drink It____

127. Hauberk . . . . Wear It____ Eat It____ Read It____ Spend It____ Drive It____ Fly It____ Drink It____

128. Roulade . . . . Wear It____ Eat It____ Read It____ Spend It____ Drive It____ Fly It____ Drink It____

129. Pierce Arrow . . . . . Wear It____ Eat It____ Read It____ Spend It____ Drive It____ Fly It____ Drink It____

130. Flan . . . . Wear It____ Eat It____ Read It____ Spend It____ Drive It____ Fly It____ Drink It____

131. Fustian . . . . Wear It____ Eat It____ Read It____ Spend It____ Drive It____ Fly It____ Drink It____

132. Tabard . . . . Wear It____ Eat It____ Read It____ Spend It____ Drive It____ Fly It____ Drink It____

133. Talent . . . . Wear It_____ Eat It_____ Read It_____
Spend It_____ Drive It_____ Fly It_____
Drink It_____

134. Tallit . . . . Wear It_____ Eat It_____ Read It_____
Spend It_____ Drive It_____ Fly It_____
Drink It_____

135. Kohlrabi . . . . Wear It_____ Eat It_____ Read It_____
Spend It_____ Drive It_____ Fly It_____
Drink It_____

136. Huaraches. . . . . . . Wear It_____ Eat It_____ Read It_____
Spend It_____ Drive It_____ Fly It_____
Drink It_____

137. Absinthe. . . . . Wear It_____ Eat It_____ Read It_____
Spend It_____ Drive It_____ Fly It_____
Drink It_____

138. Pulque. . . . . Wear It_____ Eat It_____ Read It_____
Spend It_____ Drive It_____ Fly It_____
Drink It_____

139. Jitney. . . . . Wear It_____ Eat It_____ Read It_____
Spend It_____ Drive It_____ Fly It_____
Drink It_____

140. Mackintosh . . . . . . Wear It_____ Eat It_____ Read It_____
Spend It_____ Drive It_____ Fly It_____
Drink It_____

141. Madeleine. . . . . Wear It_____ Eat It_____ Read It_____
Spend It_____ Drive It_____ Fly It_____
Drink It_____

142. Madeira. . . . . Wear It_____ Eat It_____ Read It_____
Spend It_____ Drive It_____ Fly It_____
Drink It_____

143. Mother Hubbard . . Wear It_____ Eat It_____ Read It_____
Spend It_____ Drive It_____ Fly It_____
Drink It_____

144. Marinara. . . . . Wear It_____ Eat It_____ Read It_____
Spend It_____ Drive It_____ Fly It_____
Drink It_____

145. Sarong . . . . Wear It____ Eat It____ Read It____
Spend It____ Drive It____ Fly It____
Drink It____

146. Fez . . . . Wear It____ Eat It____ Read It____
Spend It____ Drive It____ Fly It____
Drink It____

147. Mulligatawny . . . . . Wear It____ Eat It____ Read It____
Spend It____ Drive It____ Fly It____
Drink It____

148. Pousse-Café . . . . . . Wear It____ Eat It____ Read It____
Spend It____ Drive It____ Fly It____
Drink It____

149. Doubloon . . . . Wear It____ Eat It____ Read It____
Spend It____ Drive It____ Fly It____
Drink It____

150. Doublet . . . . Wear It____ Eat It____ Read It____
Spend It____ Drive It____ Fly It____
Drink It____

151. Geoduck . . . . Wear It____ Eat It____ Read It____
Spend It____ Drive It____ Fly It____
Drink It____

152. Hispano-Suiza . . . . Wear It____ Eat It____ Read It____
Spend It____ Drive It____ Fly It____
Drink It____

153. Lamborghini . . . . . . Wear It____ Eat It____ Read It____
Spend It____ Drive It____ Fly It____
Drink It____

154. Blini . . . . Wear It____ Eat It____ Read It____
Spend It____ Drive It____ Fly It____
Drink It____

155. Ruble . . . . Wear It____ Eat It____ Read It____
Spend It____ Drive It____ Fly It____
Drink It____

156. Rupee . . . . Wear It____ Eat It____ Read It____
Spend It____ Drive It____ Fly It____
Drink It____

157. Homily . . . . Wear It____ Eat It____ Read It____
Spend It____ Drive It____ Fly It____
Drink It____

158. Hominy . . . . Wear It____ Eat It____ Read It____
Spend It____ Drive It____ Fly It____
Drink It____

159. Deerstalker . . . . Wear It____ Eat It____ Read It____
Spend It____ Drive It____ Fly It____
Drink It____

160. Bugatti . . . . Wear It____ Eat It____ Read It____
Spend It____ Drive It____ Fly It____
Drink It____

161. Brioche . . . . Wear It____ Eat It____ Read It____
Spend It____ Drive It____ Fly It____
Drink It____

162. Citröen . . . . Wear It____ Eat It____ Read It____
Spend It____ Drive It____ Fly It____
Drink It____

163. Cassoulet . . . . Wear It____ Eat It____ Read It____
Spend It____ Drive It____ Fly It____
Drink It____

164. Benedictine . . . . Wear It____ Eat It____ Read It____
Spend It____ Drive It____ Fly It____
Drink It____

165. Cravat . . . Wear It____ Eat It____ Read It____
Spend It____ Drive It____ Fly It____
Drink It____

166. Telex . . . . Wear It____ Eat It____ Read It____
Spend It____ Drive It____ Fly It____
Drink It____

167. Linguisa . . . . Wear It____ Eat It____ Read It____
Spend It____ Drive It____ Fly It____
Drink It____

168. Duesenberg . . . . Wear It____ Eat It____ Read It____
Spend It____ Drive It____ Fly It____
Drink It____

169. Bombe . . . . Wear It____ Eat It____ Read It____
Spend It____ Drive It____ Fly It____
Drink It____

170. Dossier . . . . Wear It____ Eat It____ Read It____
Spend It____ Drive It____ Fly It____
Drink It____

171. Brassard . . . . Wear It____ Eat It____ Read It____
Spend It____ Drive It____ Fly It____
Drink It____

172. Syllabub . . . . Wear It____ Eat It____ Read It____
Spend It____ Drive It____ Fly It____
Drink It____

173. Surplice . . . . Wear It____ Eat It____ Read It____
Spend It____ Drive It____ Fly It____
Drink It____

174. Syllabus . . . . Wear It____ Eat It____ Read It____
Spend It____ Drive It____ Fly It____
Drink It____

175. Maxwell . . . . Wear It____ Eat It____ Read It____
Spend It____ Drive It____ Fly It____
Drink It____

Now that you've tested your ability to distinguish between things and their functions and purposes, you're ready to apply what you know to make rather more refined distinctions. Although some of the items in that last series of questions were surely obscure, the functions and purposes were hugely distinct. After all, you wouldn't want to be reading a novel, a biography, or a newspaper story and so totally confuse what was going on that you imagined someone drinking a surplice or flying a Grignolino.

The American poet e. e. cummings, unknown to legions of American high school and college graduates, wrote, "All ignorance toboggans into know/and trudges up to ignorance again." In taking the quite human toboggan ride from ignorance to know, one must be willing to trudge the hills. The exhilaration in the ride, however, makes it worth the climb. Applying the knowledge validates the difficulty it may take to acquire it.

It sounds obvious to say that we use our knowledge to

think. Names and dates give tangibility, give symbolic reality to the past and to the present, provide us with the fragile and fallible tools of understanding. But there is a notion popular in some educational circles that absorbing facts, dates, names, and data is an empty exercise, a kind of intellectual fascism, a process deadening to the imagination and destructive to individuality and creativity.

No buzzword is more feared in educational circles than the phrase *rote learning*. We can't have that, of course. The positive opposite of rote learning is *critical thinking*, which is good. Yet it should be pointed out that critical thinking is a redundancy. How would one think uncritically? That wouldn't be thinking at all. Advocates of "critical thinking" apparently haven't practiced what they preach. And meanwhile, isn't it first necessary to gather the tools necessary for thoughtful decisions?

It's not important, runs the argument, that students know *when* the Civil War was fought, nor is it important for them to know the principal players in that drama. It is only important that they know the reasons why. But how can you have one thing without the other? How can any decent understanding of apartheid, for example, be formulated in the absence of knowledge about the location of South Africa, its historical roots, its economic fundament, its long cast of heroes and villains?

Rote learning is seen as mindless, a meaningless stockpiling of data retained only long enough to be regurgitated at test time. But is rote learning, properly defined and applied, really that mindless? Properly taught, geography can inflame the imagination, stimulate thinking, widen the sense of possibility. Properly taught, history can reduce the isolation of being human, can allow us to know that our joys and sorrows are not unique, can point out directions, show us dangers in the path ahead. Properly taught, literature can tell us who we are personally, nationally, globally. And all of that begins with the naming of things. It *begins* there, and then we trudge the hill some more.

As illustration, the following section goes beyond the simpler distinctions and discriminations required in the earlier sections of this chapter's test. Knowing and thinking become more nearly equal partners in this one. Here you must employ what you know in order to think with it.

Each of the following questions is comprised of a series of people, events, places, or things. One of the items in each series is in some way distinct from the others. First you recognize and identify, then you must reason the distinction.

TEST 3C
WHICH OF THESE THINGS IS NOT LIKE THE OTHER?

176. a. Thor   b. Zeus   c. Svengali   d. Quetzalcoatl
e. Wakan-Tanka   f. Ra

177. a. Billy Budd   b. Tom Jones   c. Zebulon Pike
d. Tristram Shandy   e. Martin Chuzzlewit

178. a. Hester Prynne   b. Anna Karenina   c. Madame
Bovary   d. Dolly Madison   e. Jane Eyre

179. a. Kurosawa   b. Truffaut   c. Griffith   d. Coppola
e. Hickok   f. Hitchcock   g. Spielberg

180. a. Julia Child   b. Meryl Streep   c. Theda Bara
d. Lillian Gish   e. Greta Garbo

181. a. Davy Crockett   b. Daniel Boone   c. Johnny Appleseed   d. Natty Bumpo   e. Captain John Smith

182. a. Winston Churchill   b. Benito Mussolini   c. Joseph
Stalin   d. Franklin Roosevelt   e. Charles de Gaulle

183. a. Stephen Biko   b. P. W. Botha   c. Desmond Tutu
d. Nelson Mandela

184. a. Saladin   b. Othello   c. Hamlet   d. Romeo   e. King
Lear   f. Iago

185. a. Billy Sunday   b. Elmer Gantry   c. Jimmy Swaggart
d. Jim Bakker   e. Father Divine   f. Oral Roberts

186. a. Brie   b. Belize   c. Gouda   d. Camembert   e. Feta
f. Limburger

187. a. Tlingit   b. Arapahoe   c. Masai   d. Paiute
e. Choctaw   f. Piegan

188. a. Hereford   b. Jersey   c. Guernsey   d. Manx
e. Longhorn

189. a. Shaker   b. Quaker   c. Anabaptist   d. Amish
e. Arbitrager   f. Pentecostal

190. a. Melvin Laird   b. Percy Shelley   c. Caspar Wein-
berger   d. Edwin Stanton   e. Frank Carlucci

191. a. Palomino   b. Mastiff   c. Appaloosa   d. Arabian
e. Morgan

192. a. Django Reinhardt   b. Andres Segovia   C. Eric Clapton   d. Luciano Pavarotti   e. Chet Atkins

193. a. e. e. cummings   b. J. P. Morgan   c. T. S. Eliot
d. W. H. Auden   e. A. E. Housman

194. a. Mekong Delta   b. Khe Sanh   c. My Lai   d. Saigon
e. Gulf of Tonkin   f. Inchon

195. a. Alexander Pope   b. John Donne   c. Mathew Brady
d. John Keats   f. William Blake

196. a. Jane Austen   b. George Eliot   c. Charlotte Brontë
d. Virginia Woolf   e. Sally Ride

197. a. Titian   b. Tintoretto   c. Tertullian   d. Tamayo
e. Toulouse-Lautrec

198. a. Fer-de-lance   b. Oryx   c. Gnu   d. Springbok
e. Wildebeest

199. a. Puccini   b. Linguini   c. Tartini   d. Vivaldi

200. a. George McClellan   b. William T. Sherman
c. U. S. Grant   d. Thomas Jackson   e. George A. Custer

TEST 3A ANSWERS

Not long ago I had occasion to teach a class of third- and fourth-grade children. I expected the sort of indifference I so often find in my college classes. It surprised me, then, when every question I asked prompted a little forest of waving hands and a chorus of "I know, I know, pick me." The joy of knowing was apparent on those young faces. That joy of knowing survives in adults, but we bury it under years of cumulative uncertainty and insecurity provided by years of fragmented and intimidating teaching and learning, which often is surprisingly light in content, dampens our quite natural enthusiasm to know things, and replaces knowing with a dubious mastery of skills.

The tests found here are not for teachers, record books, transcripts, potential employers. These tests allow you to take your own measure, to accept or reject the need to know certain things, to excel for your own pleasure, or to fail as a means of diagnosing what you don't know. Along the way, you just might rediscover what is and what is not important to you. An education, after all, should enable you to make such critical decisions.

1. George Sand was *Female*. Pen name of Amandine-Aurore-Lucile Dupin Dudevant (1804–1876), French novelist.

2. Flannery O'Connor was *Female*. Mary Flannery O'Conner (1925–1964), American writer.

3. Evelyn Waugh was *Male*. Evelyn Arthur St. John Waugh (1903–1966), English novelist.

4. Hecuba was *Female*. In Greek mythology, the queen of Troy.

5. Isak Dinesen was *Female*. Pen name of Karen Christence Dinesen (1885–1962), Danish writer.

6. Marion Morrison was *Male*. Real name of John Wayne (1907–1979), American movie actor.

7. E. B. White was *Male*. Elwin Brooks White (1899–1985), American writer.

8. Babe Didrikson was *Female*. Mildred Didrikson Zaharias (1914–1956), U.S. athlete, especially known for golf.

9. Camille Saint-Saëns was *Male*. Charles-Camille Saint-Saens (1835–1921), French composer.

10. Sappho was *Female*. Sixth century B.C. Greek lyric poet.

11. Yo-Yo Ma (1955–) is *Male*. Cellist.

12. Reza Pahlevi was *Male*. Reza Khan (1878–1944), Shah of Iran. Succeeded by his son, Mohammad Reza Pahlevi (1919–1980).

13. Ovid was *Male*. Publius Ovidius Naso (43 B.C.–A.D. 17), Roman poet.

14. Vidkun Quisling was *Male*. Vidkun Abraham Lauritz Jonsson Quisling (1887–1945), Norwegian facist, traitor.

15. Carson McCullers was *Female*. Lula Carson Smith McCullers (1917–1967), American novelist.

16. Osceola (ca. 1804–1838) was *Male*. American Seminole Indian leader.

17. George Eliot was *Female*. Pen name of Mary Ann (Marian) Evans (1819–1880), English novelist.

18. A. A. Milne was *Male*. Alan Alexander Milne (1882–1956), English writer.

19. Stevie Smith was *Female*. Pen name of Florence Margaret Smith (1902–1971), English writer.

20. Rainer Maria Rilke was *Male*. (1875–1926), German poet.

21. Francis Marion was *Male*. Also known as The Swamp Fox (ca. 1732–1795), commander during the American Revolution.

22. Yasuhiro Nakasone (1918–) is *Male*. Japanese political leader and former prime minister.

23. Sun Yat-sen was *Male*. Also known as Sun Chung-shan (1866–1925), Chinese statesman and revolutionary leader.

24. Glenn Close (1947–) is *Female*. Contemporary American film actress.

25. Vachel Lindsay was *Male*. Nicholas Vachel Lindsay (1879–1931), American poet.

26. Kobo Abe is *Male*. Kimifusa Abe (1924–), Japanese poet and novelist.

27. Sacagawea (ca. 1786–1812) was *Female*. American Indian interpreter and guide, member of the Shoshone tribe.

28. Osiris is/was *Male*. In Egyptian legend, the god of the underworld.

29. Ellery Queen was *Male*. Pseudonym of cousins Frederic Dannay (1905–1982) and Manfred B. Lee (1905–1971), American mystery writers. Ellery Queen is also the name of the detective character they created.

30. Alice Cooper is *Male*. Vincent Furnier (1945–), American punk rock singer.

31. Fra Filippo Lippi (ca. 1406–1469) was *Male*. Florentine painter.

32. Toshiro Mifune is *Male*. (1920–), Japanese actor.

33. Flo Ziegfeld was *Male*. Florenz Ziegfeld (1869–1932), American theatrical producer.

34. The Valkyries were *Female*. In Norse mythology, maidens of Odin who conducted the souls of slain heros to Valhalla.

35. Joan Miró (1893–1983) was *Male*. Spanish painter.

36. Pygmalion was *Male*. In Greek legend, a sculptor who fell

in love with his statue of a maiden whom Aphrodite brought to life at his prayer.

37. Piaf was *Female*. Edith Giovanna Gassion (1915–1963), French singer.

38. Narcissus was *Male*. In Greek mythology, a handsome youth who fell in love with his own reflection in a spring.

39. Tecumseh (ca. 1768–1813) was *Male*. Shawnee Indian chief.

40. Pol Pot is *Male*. Saloth Sar (1928–), infamous Cambodian political leader. Organizer of the Khmer Rouge.

41. Saint Frances Xavier Cabrini was *Female*. Also known as Mother Cabrini (1850–1917), Italian-born American nun. First American citizen to be canonized.

42. Somerset Maugham was *Male*. William Somerset Maugham (1874–1965), English author.

43. Amedeo Modigliani was *Male*. (1884–1920), Italian painter.

44. Jean Lafitte (ca. 1780–ca. 1826) was *Male*. French pirate.

45. Jeane Duane Jordon Kirkpatrick (1926–) is *Female*. American diplomat and educator. Former ambassador to the United Nations.

46. Bashō was *Male*. Munefusa Matsuo (1644–1694), Japanese poet.

47. Sandy Koufax is *Male*. Sanford Koufax (1935–), American baseball player.

48. Liliuokalani was *Female*. Also known as Lydia Paki Lilioukalani and Liliu Kamakaeha (1838–1917), queen of the Hawaiian Islands, 1891–1893.

49. Ceres is/was *Female*. In Roman mythology, goddess of agriculture.

50. Joyce Kilmer was *Male*. Alfred Joyce Kilmer (1886–1918), American poet.

51. W. C. Handy was *Male*. William Christopher Handy (1873–1958), American jazz musician and composer, called "Father of the Blues."

52. Chiang Kai-shek was *Male*. Chiang Chung-cheng (1887–1975), Chinese general and political leader.

53. Odin was *Male*. Chief deity of Norse mythology.

54. Aesop was *Male*. Real or legendary Greek author. Credited with the authorship of *Aesop's Fables*.

55. Svetlana Alliluyeva (1925–) is *Female*. Daughter of Josef Stalin.

56. The Furies were *Female*. In Greek and Roman mythology, three vengeful goddesses/spirits with snakes for hair.

57. Nebuchadnezzar (?–562 B.C.) was *Male*. Babylonian king.

58. Shiva is/was *Male*. One of the gods of the Hindu trinity; represents destruction.

59. E. Power Biggs was *Male*. Edward George Power-Biggs (1906–1977), British born American organist.

60. Valéry Giscard d'Estaing (1926–) is *Male*. President of France, 1974–1981.

61. Countee Cullen (1903–1946) was *Male*. American poet.

62. Hammurabi (?–1750 B.C.) was *Male*. Babylonian king.

63. Fran Tarkenton is *Male*. Francis Asbury Tarkenton (1940–), American football player.

64. Sun Myung Moon is *Male*. Reverend Sun Myung Moon (1920–), Korean evangelist, convicted of income tax fraud in U.S. in 1982.

65. Imamu Amiri Baraka is *Male*. LeRoi Jones (1934–), American poet and playwright.

66. Molech was *Male*. Also known as Moloch. Biblical god of fire to whom children were sacrificed.

67. B. F. Skinner is *Male*. Burrhus Frederic Skinner (1904–), American psychologist.

68. Kahlil Gibran was *Male*. Jubran Kahlil Jubran (1883–1931), Syrian poet who lived in the United States.

69. Saladin was *Male*. Salah ad-Din Yusuf ibn Ayyub (ca. 1137–1193), Muslim sultan and hero.

70. Circe was *Female*. Greek mythology. In Homer's *Odyssey*, an enchantress who turned men into swine.

71. Hideki Tojo (1884–1948) was *Male*. Japanese soldier and political leader. Hanged as a war criminal.

72. Sirhan Sirhan is *Male*. Sirhan Bishara Sirhan (1944–), Palestinian born assassin of Robert F. Kennedy.

73. Corazon Aquino is *Female*. Corazon Conjuangco Aquino (1933–), became president of the Philippines in 1986.

74. Yukio Mishima was *Male*. Pseudonym of Hiraoka Kimitake (1925–1970), Japanese writer who committed hari-kari as a public protest against the Westernization of Japan.

75. Benazir Bhutto (1953–) is *Female*. Prime Minister of Pakistan.

TEST 3B ANSWERS

76. Plaice: *Eat It*. An American or European flatfish.

77. Lorgnette: *Wear It*. Pair of eyeglasses attached to a handle.

78. Snood: *Wear It*. Baglike net for hair worn at back of the head.

79. Ouzo: *Drink It*. Anise-flavored Greek cordial.

80. Dashiki: *Wear It*. Loose-fitting, brightly colored tunic.

81. Pfennig: *Spend It*. German unit of currency.

82. Codpiece: *Wear It*. Flap fastened over the front opening of men's breeches (fifteenth and sixteenth centuries).

83. Fernet Branca: *Drink It*. Bitter Italian liquor.

84. Sopwith Camel: *Fly It*. British aircraft used in World War I.

85. Villanelle: *Read It*. A form of poetry.

86. Farthing: *Spend It*. A former unit of British currency equal to one-fourth of a penny.

87. Burnoose: *Wear It*. A long, hooded cloak.

88. Gherkin: *Eat It*. A variety of small cucumbers used to make pickles.

89. Mantilla: *Wear It*. A woman's headpiece, often made of lace.

90. Jerkin: *Wear It*. A short, close-fitting vest.

91. Stuka: *Fly It*. World War II German fighter plane.

92. Shoat: *Eat It*. A young hog.

93. Slivovitz: *Drink It*. A kind of plum brandy.

94. Stutz-Bearcat: *Drive It*. American sportscar, ca. 1914.

95. Potboiler: *Read It*. A piece of inferior writing, usually done just for money.

96. Rondelet: *Read It*. A form of poetry.

97. Furbelow: *Wear It*. A ruffle or flounce.

98. Dhoti: *Wear It*. A Hindu loincloth.

99. Chorizo: *Eat It*. A highly seasoned sausage often used in Mexican cooking.

100. Chaddar: *Wear It*. A shawl worn by women in India.

101. Dry Sack: *Drink It*. Dry sherry wine.

102. Bodice Ripper: *Read It*. A kind of romance novel.

103. Spruce Goose: *Fly It*. Experimental wooden aircraft designed by Howard Hughes.

104. Miter: *Wear It*. A religious headdress.

105. Montrachet: *Drink It*. White wine.

106. Finnan Haddie: *Eat It*. Smoked haddock.

107. Farinaceous: *Eat It*. Something made from flour or meal.

108. Babushka: *Wear It*. Woman's head-scarf that ties under chin.

109. Grignolino: *Drink It*. An Italian red wine.

110. Stilton: *Eat It*. A semi-hard English blue cheese.

111. Bolero: *Wear It*. A short, open-fronted jacket. (Also, a Spanish dance.)

112. Cous-cous: *Eat It*. A North African dish made of cracked wheat grain.

113. Kirtle: *Wear It*. A man's tunic or coat; a woman's dress or skirt.

114. Krona: *Spend It*. A unit of currency in Sweden (or Iceland if spelled with an accent over the "o").

115. Pince-nez: *Wear It*. Eyeglasses kept in place by a spring gripping the bridge of the nose.

116. Roman à clef: *Read It*. A novel in which real people appear under fictitious names.

117. Ort: *Eat It*—or not, since it's an uneaten morsel of food.

118. Bel Paese: *Eat It*. A soft, creamy cheese.

119. Haiku: *Read It*. A form of Japanese verse.

120. Caftan: *Wear It*. A long-sleeved, full-length garment.

121. Lira: *Spend It*. A unit of Italian or Turkish currency.

122. Novella: *Read It*. A short novel.

123. Redingote: *Wear It*. A long coat.

124. Retsina: *Drink It*. A Greek wine flavored with pine resin.

125. Spad: *Fly It*. A French aircraft in World War I.

126. Karmann Ghia: *Drive It*. A German two-seater convertible.

127. Hauberk: *Wear It*. Medieval armor usually made of chain mail.

128. Roulade: *Eat It*. German meat roll.

129. Pierce Arrow: *Drive It*. Prestigious American car ca. 1903–1938.

130. Flan: *Eat It*. Custard tart.

131. Fustian: *Wear It*. Thick cotton cloth with a short nap.

132. Tabard: *Wear It*. Loose jacket of heavy material.

133. Talent: *Spend It*. Large unit of weight or money used in ancient Greece, Rome, and the Middle East.

134. Tallit: *Wear It*. Jewish prayer shawl.

135. Kohlrabi: *Eat It*. Vegetable related to cabbage.

136. Huaraches: *Wear It*. Spanish/Mexican flat, woven leather sandals.

137. Absinthe: *Drink It*. Bitter, green liquor with the flavor of wormwood and anise.

138. Pulque: *Drink It*. Fermented Mexican drink made from the juice of an agave.

139. Jitney: *Spend It* or *Drive It*. Old slang term for a five-cent coin or a small bus or car.

140. Mackintosh: *Wear It*. Raincoat.

141. Madeleine: *Eat It*. Small, rich cupcake.

142. Madeira: *Drink It*. A type of wine.

143. Mother Hubbard: *Wear It*. Full, loose gown for women.

144. Marinara: *Eat It*. A seasoned tomato sauce.

145. Sarong: *Wear It*. Garment made by wrapping a long piece of cloth around the body like a skirt or dress.

146. Fez: *Wear It*. Conical felt hat tapering to a flat crown, of Turkish origin.

147. Mulligatawny: *Eat It*. East Indian meat soup or stew.

148. Pousse-Café: *Drink It*. A drink made of several layers of different liqueurs.

149. Doubloon: *Spend It*. Obsolete Spanish gold coin.

150. Doublet: *Wear It*. Close-fitting sleeved or sleeveless jacket worn by men during the fourteenth through sixteenth centuries.

151. Geoduck: *Eat It*. A very large clam of the Pacific Northwest.

152. Hispano-Suiza: *Drive It*. Car of both Spanish and French manufacture (1904–1944).

153. Lamborghini: *Drive It*. Italian sportscar introduced in 1963.

154. Blini: *Eat It*. Small, thin pancakes.

155. Ruble: *Spend It*. Monetary unit of the Soviet Union.

156. Rupee: *Spend It*. Monetary unit of India, Pakistan, and Ceylon.

157. Homily: *Read It*. Sermon.

158. Hominy: *Eat It*. Dry corn.

159. Deerstalker: *Wear It*. Hunter's cap.

160. Bugatti: *Drive It*. Italian racing and touring car.

161. Brioche: *Eat It*. Light, rich roll.

162. Citröen: *Drive It*. French car.

163. Cassoulet: *Eat It*. Casserole made of beans and meat or poultry.

164. Benedictine: *Drink It*. Liqueur containing herbs and spices made by Benedictine monks in France.

165. Cravat: *Wear It*. A necktie or scarf.

166. Telex: *Read It*. A message sent by a teletypewriter (or the machine itself)

167. Linguisa: *Eat It*. A spicy sausage

168. Duesenberg: *Drive It*. American racing and touring car

169. Bombe: *Eat It*. A round molded dessert

170. Dossier: *Read It*. A collection of documents assembled on a particular person or subject

171. Brassard: *Wear It*. Armor for the upper arm or an arm band that identifies the wearer in a particular way

172. Syllabub: *Drink It* or *Eat It*. A sweet drink or dessert made of milk and wine or cider and beaten to a froth

173. Surplice: *Wear It*. A loose-fitting white garment worn by clergy or choir

174. Syllabus: *Read It*. A summary or outline of the content of a course of study

175. Maxwell: *Drive It*. Early twentieth-century American car

TEST 3C ANSWERS

176. c. *Svengali*, fictional character in the novel *Trilby* by George du Maurier, and in the movie *Svengali* (1931). All the rest are gods

177. c. *Zebulon Pike* (1779–1813), American explorer. All the rest are fictional characters

178. d. *Dolly Madison* (1768–1849), wife of fourth president of the United States. All the rest are fictional characters

179. e. *Hickok*, James Butler (1837–1876), also known as Wild Bill Hickok. All the rest are film directors

180. a. *Julia Child* (1912–), famous cook. All the rest are actresses

181. d. *Natty Bumpo*, fictional character, not an authentic American hero

182. b. *Benito Mussolini* (1883–1945), Axis dictator, not one of the Allies in World War II

183. b. *P. W. Botha* (1916–), white South African champion of apartheid, not a black South African resistance leader

184. a. *Saladin* (1137?–1193), Muslim warrior and sultan of Egypt. All the rest are Shakespearean characters.

185. b. *Elmer Gantry*, fictional evangelist in Sinclair Lewis novel of the same name. The rest are real evangelists.

186. b. *Belize*, a country in Central America. The rest are cheeses.

187. c. *Masai*, an African tribal group. The rest are American Indian Tribes.

188. d. *Manx*, a cat. The rest are cows.

189. e. *Arbitrager*, a dealer in money. The others worship God.

190. b. *Percy Shelley* (1792–1822), English poet. All the rest have been U.S. Secretaries of Defense.

191. b. *Mastiff*, a dog. The others are horses.

192. d. *Luciano Pavarotti* (1935–), Italian tenor. The others play guitar.

193. b. *J. P. Morgan* (1837–1913), U.S. financier. The rest are poets.

194. f. *Inchon*, a city in South Korea. The rest are in Vietnam.

195. c. *Mathew Brady* (ca. 1823–1896), U.S. Civil War photographer. The rest are English poets.

196. d. *Sally Ride* (1951–), U.S. astronaut. The others are English writers.

197. c. *Tertullian* (A.D. 155–220), Ecclesiastical writer and one of the founders of the Catholic Church. The others are painters.

198. a. *Fer-de-lance*, a snake. The rest are mammals and ruminants.

199. b. *Linguini*, a pasta. The others are composers.

200. d. *Thomas Jackson* (1824–1863), also known as "Stonewall" Jackson. Confederate general in U.S. Civil War. The others were Yankees.

SCORING

Although many of the items tested here are obscure or at least not commonly known, the scoring is exacting for this chapter because the knowledge being tested is both primary and pragmatic, requiring the ability to distinguish between men and women and between the functions of things. And even though gender may not be the most important or significant fact about the characters in the first part of this test, many of their accomplishments or much of their significance can be traced to gender. In any event, the ability to draw the distinction is directly related to how much you know.

161–200: Congratulations. You have considerable knowledge of the kind that allows you to make important distinctions. You're an ace distinguisher.

121–160: You've demonstrated that you know more than you don't know about important differences.

81–120: Somewhat marginal. You could have scored in this range by merely guessing. If you didn't guess, then take solace in knowing that, while there is much you don't know, there is also much that you do know. And there is all that opportunity now to fill in the gaps.

80 or less: This was a frustrating chapter for you. You'll want to learn all you can to avoid future frustration.

CHAPTER FOUR

A TEST OF THE *TIMES*

Open the pages of the *New York Times* (or any other major newspaper) and the names come tumbling out in an avalanche of people, places, and things writers and editors assume you know. Walter Benjamin, a German literary critic, said, "When we read a book, the book is reading us." The same can be said of reading newspapers. Unless we bring a certain body of knowledge to our reading, the newspaper is likely to read us as deficient in the knowledge necessary to evaluate and interpret the flood of information and opinion the paper delivers.

As the nation's premiere news source, the *New York Times* serves as a key voice for collecting and disseminating the American view of the world. It would seem reasonable to assume that any college student (or high school graduate) could read and understand most of what the *New York Times* publishes. Such expectations turn out to be great expectations in view of current levels of common knowledge. Fragmented educations and equally fragmented broadcast news presentations have combined to produce a nation of people who cannot understand the world they inhabit. Having taken several classes of college students through the *New York Times*, I can say with certainty that both the vocabulary and the common references employed by *Times* writers are bewildering and virtually indecipherable to most of today's high school grads.

People can always look up what they don't know, can't they? Yes, of course, they can. But how many people are likely to take the time to look up the hundreds of references and allusions readily found in any edition of any major newspaper? The very act of reading becomes frustrating and unpleasant when there is no shared context because the reader doesn't know enough. According to polls, most college age students seldom, if ever, read a daily newspaper, seldom, if ever, watch television news. This is perhaps why so many of my students had never heard of Mike Wallace when he arrived to do his report on my test of general knowledge. In any event, the reason for this reluctance to read or watch news probably can be traced to the difficulty it causes students when they cannot bring enough to the act of viewing and reading to allow them to make sense of it. I can think of no more significant condemnation of this country's educational system.

Last year a Japanese student enrolled in my Introduction to Literature class. As is the case with many students, poetry was giving her great difficulty. She read diligently, pondered mightily, but the metaphors and the cultural allusions—let alone the vocabulary—made reading poetry in English a quite understandable struggle. Finally, in exasperation, she wrote, "Reading with guessing is not easy." She could have been speaking for a great many Americans, who for the same reason have given up reading newspapers. Students across the country have been found to be ignorant of such commonly used terms as *apartheid, contra, SDI, glasnost,* and *detente.* In fact, some of my teaching colleagues are unclear about some of these terms. Even such a highly profiled world leader as Mikhail Gorbachev was misidentified by nearly one-third of a California college *journalism* class. Some of them thought he was a ballet dancer.

The tests in this chapter are made up of people, places, and things culled from a single Sunday edition of the *New York Times* or from similar editions of the *Chicago Tribune* or the *San Francisco Chronicle.* Many of the items found in these tests were used in the papers without clarifying or explanatory copy. The writers and editors assumed the readers would know. After all, newspapers don't come with footnotes. Should they do otherwise? Should writers and editors begin to write to an audience presumed devoid of any shared heritage or knowledge? Or should we expect and even demand more of ourselves, our society, and our schools?

Take the following test and find out if you know enough to read the *Times* without guessing. We'll begin with a game of reconstruction. In the first part of the test, items from the various sections of the paper have been pulled out of context. Your job is to restore that context. In what section of the paper would the following people most likely be found? What sphere of human endeavor are they most associated with? (All items in this test were culled from the September 4, 1988, Sunday edition of the *New York Times.*)

TEST 4A
TIMES, ONE

IN WHICH SECTION WOULD EACH OF THE FOLLOWING PEOPLE MOST LIKELY BE MENTIONED? PUT A CHECK MARK NEXT TO THE APPROPRIATE CHOICE.

1. Ford Madox Ford . . . . . . Art____ Politics____ Business____
   Entertainment____ Sports____
   Literature____

2. George Grosz . . . . Art____ Politics____ Business____
   Entertainment____ Sports____
   Literature____

3. Steffi Graf . . . . Art____ Politics____ Business____
   Entertainment____ Sports____
   Literature____

4. Clifford Odets . . . . Art____ Politics____ Business____
   Entertainment____ Sports____
   Literature____

5. Augusto Pinochet . . . . . Art____ Politics____ Business____
   Entertainment____ Sports____
   Literature____

6. Ed Koch . . . . Art____ Politics____ Business____
   Entertainment____ Sports____
   Literature____

7. Henry Moore . . . . Art____ Politics____ Business____
   Entertainment____ Sports____
   Literature____

8. José Greco . . . . Art____ Politics____ Business____
   Entertainment____ Sports____
   Literature____

9. Josef Stalin . . . . Art____ Politics____ Business____
   Entertainment____ Sports____
   Literature____

10. Mario Cuomo . . . . Art____ Politics____ Business____
    Entertainment____ Sports____
    Literature____

11. Phyllis Schlafly . . . . . . Art____ Politics____ Business____
Entertainment____ Sports____
Literature____

12. Brian Bosworth . . . . . . Art____ Politics____ Business____
Entertainment____ Sports____
Literature____

13. Thomas P. "Tip"
O'Neill . . . . Art____ Politics____ Business____
Entertainment____ Sports____
Literature____

14. River Phoenix . . . . Art____ Politics____ Business____
Entertainment____ Sports____
Literature____

15. Reverend Louis
Farrakhan. . . . . Art____ Politics____ Business____
Entertainment____ Sports____
Literature____

16. Darryl Zanuck . . . . . . Art____ Politics____ Business____
Entertainment____ Sports____
Literature____

17. Oscar Wilde. . . . . Art____ Politics____ Business____
Entertainment____ Sports____
Literature____

18. Tracy Chapman. . . . . . Art____ Politics____ Business____
Entertainment____ Sports____
Literature____

19. Dwight Gooden. . . . . . Art____ Politics____ Business____
Entertainment____ Sports____
Literature____

20. William Casey. . . . . . . Art____ Politics____ Business____
Entertainment____ Sports____
Literature____

That should have been fairly easy. Now, for the next leg of our journey through the *Times*, try these words, phrases, and initials that *Times* writers assumed you knew. This is a define or identify quiz.

TEST 4B
TIMES, TOO

21. *CIA* stands for the _____

22. *GAO* stands for the _____

23. *NOW* stands for the _____

24. *ERA* stands for the _____

25. *Redux* means _____

26. *Nirvana* is _____

27. *Golgotha* is _____

28. The *id* is _____

29. A *junta* is _____

30. A *tête-à-tête* is _____

The next set of questions were drawn from the August 21, 1988 Sunday edition of the *Chicago Tribune*. Let's see if common knowledge is a bit more common out in the heartland.

TEST 4C
TRIBUNAL

IDENTIFY THE FOLLOWING BY SUPPLYING THE MISSING NAMES OR IDENTIFYING INFORMATION.

31. Patty Hearst _____

32. Perestroika _____

33. Graceland _____

34. *Izvestia* _____

35. The Gipper _____

36. _____ played the Gipper in the motion picture *Knute Rockne, All American*.

37. "Papa" is the nickname by which _____ is remembered.

38. Dagwood Bumstead is married to _____

39. E.T. stands for _____

40. Ring Lardner was a famous _____

41. Daddy Warbucks has a paternal relationship with _____

_____

42. Dith Pran was made known to the world in the movie

about his experiences entitled _____

43. Bess Myerson made the Chicago paper because of her

fame as a former _____ who was indicted for _____

44. Rube Goldberg is remembered for _____

45. Mel Blanc is best known as the voice of _____

46. *Couch Potato* is a term to describe _____

47. *American Gothic* is a famous _____

created by _____

48. PLO stands for _____

49. Buddy Holly is best known for the song _____

50. *La Prensa* is the often beleaguered _____ of this

Latin American country _____

Now we'll sample some of what we might find in a typical Sunday edition of the *San Francisco Chronicle/Examiner*, this one from October 16, 1988.

TEST 4D
WEST COAST

AGAIN, SUPPLY THE MISSING NAMES OR IDENTIFYING INFORMATION.

51. IHS, emblazoned on religious vestments, means _____ _____

52. Charles de Gaulle was once _____

53. Black Monday, October 19, 1987, is remembered as the

day _____

54. A trade deficit occurs when a nation _____ more

than it _____

55. Scotland Yard is to Great Britain as _____
is to the United States.

56. Deng Xiaoping is _____

57. Henry Cisneros is the well-known mayor of _____

58. Crips and Bloods are _____

59. "It ain't over till it's over," is one of the pithy comments

attributed to Yogi Berra, who is also fondly remembered as

a _____

60. Midas fever is more commonly called _____

61. An IRA is an _____

62. But a member of the IRA belongs to the _____

_____

63. A member of the NRA pays dues to the _____

_____

64. The Fab Four were _____, _____, _____,

and _____ who were collectively known as _____

65. The escudo is the base currency of _____

66. In the Gobi Desert of Outer Mongolia, you might find

yurts, which are _____

67. *Treasure Island* was just one of many novels by _____

_____

68. *Water Music* is the work of composer _____

69. Younger readers might never have seen an Edsel and

therefore might not know it is a _____

70. Joyce Carol Oates is a prolific _____

71. A Freudian slip is _____

72. Oliver North held the rank of _____ and is

best known from the _____

73. The Helga Pictures garnered considerable publicity for

_____

74. Dian Fossey is known for her work with _____

75. "Bird" is the nickname of American jazz great _____

76. Jerry Garcia is the leader of this long-surviving rock 'n' roll

band _____

77. *Hedda Gabler* is a play by _____

78. Amnesty International is an organization concerned with

the problems of _____

79. Much discussed in the 1988 presidential campaign, the

ACLU is the _____

80. *Die Meistersinger, Parsifal, Siegfried,* and *The Ring* are

among the works of _____

Now that we've completed the briefest sampling of references and allusions in newspapers from the East Coast to the West, it should be easy to see just how much we are expected to bring to the relatively mundane act of reading a newspaper. To round out this sampling, let's return to the Big Apple for one last test of what you know of those things that fairly routinely appear in print. The following items are but a few of the thousands that appeared in the September 1, 1988, issue. If you feel you've done poorly so far in this test, this is your last shot at redemption; if you're doing well, this is an opportunity to finish with a flourish. In any case, whether you knew many or few, you now know where your knowledge has been lacking. If your interest dictates, you can now find out more. The answers might explain why those writers and editors presumed on your time and knowledge in the first place.

TEST 4E
TIMES, THREE

81. The Mekong Delta is in _____

82. Kent State is in Ohio. Unfortunately, it is best remembered

as _____

83. When something is described as Wordsworthian it refers

to _____ who was an English romantic _____

84. Wilhelm Reich is remembered for his work in the field of

_____

85. "Clean for Gene" was a slogan associated with Eugene

McCarthy, who was a _____ in 1968.

86. Jack Ruby went down in history as _____

87. A Zionist is one who believes in _____

88. Emma Goldman is historically important because of her

activities as a _____

89. Art Deco was a popular style in the decade of the _____

90. The Greenhouse Effect has many people worried. It is the

theory that _____

due to _____

91. Dwight Yoakam, Randy Travis, and k. d. lang have all

had recent and notable success in the field of _____

92. Kim Philby was an infamous _____

93. Tom Hayden was a _____ in the 1960s, became a _____ in the 1980s, but perhaps became better known as the husband of _____

94. Jean Nicolas Arthur Rimbaud was a _____

95. Colorization is _____

96. Martha Graham is famous in the world of _____

97. H. L. Mencken is remembered for his work as _____

98. "Shoeless" Joe Jackson's memory was tarnished in connection with _____

99. Boris Pasternak and Aleksandr Solzhenitsyn are both known worldwide as _____

100. L. L. Bean is a name associated with _____

Had you been reading any of these or comparable Sunday papers, your reading would have either been enhanced or diminished by what you did or did not bring with you when you picked up the paper. Each day's edition of nearly every paper in the country presumes that we are sufficiently knowledgeable about the past, art, literature, politics, and geography. Do they presume too much? Check your answers to find out.

TEST 4A ANSWERS

1. *Literature*. Ford Madox Ford (1873–1939), English novelist.

2. *Art*. George Grosz (1893–1959), German-born, American artist.

3. *Sports*. Steffi Graf, (1969–) contemporary women's tennis star.

4. *Literature*. Clifford Odets (1906–1963), American playwright.

5. *Politics*. Augusto Pinochet (1915–), deposed Chilean dictator.

6. *Politics*. Ed Koch (1924–), former Mayor of New York.

7. *Art*. Henry Moore (1898–1986), English sculptor.

8. *Entertainment*. José Greco (1918–), flamenco dancer.

9. *Politics*. Josef Stalin (1879–1953), Soviet political leader.

10. *Politics*. Mario Cuomo (1932–), Governor of New York.

11. *Politics*. Phyllis Schlafly (1924–), conservative political activist.

12. *Sports*. Brian Bosworth (1965–), football player, Seattle Seahawks.

13. *Politics*. Thomas P. "Tip" O'Neill (1912–), Democrat, former Speaker of the House.

14. *Entertainment*. River Phoenix (1970–), movie actor.

15. *Politics*. Reverend Louis Farrakhan (1933–), controversial black religious leader.

16. *Entertainment*. Darryl Zanuck (1902–1979), movie mogul.

17. *Literature*. Oscar Wilde (1854–1900), Irish poet/dramatist.

18. *Entertainment*. Tracy Chapman (1964–), contemporary singer/songwriter.

19. *Sports*. Dwight Gooden (1964–), baseball player.

20. *Politics*. William Casey (1913–1987), head of CIA.

TEST 4B ANSWERS

21. CIA stands for the Central Intelligence Agency.

22. GAO stands for the General Accounting Office.

23. NOW stands for the National Organization for Women.

24. ERA stands for the Equal Rights Amendment.

25. Redux is Latin for "brought back, revived, restored."

26. Nirvana is, in Buddhist belief, the state of perfect blessedness. It has come to mean any condition of bliss.

27. Golgotha is "the place of the skulls," where Jesus was crucified.

28. The id is a psychoanalytic term to define the part of the

psyche that is driven by instinct and desire. In Freudian theory, the id is counterbalanced by the ego.

29. A junta is, literally, an assembly or council, but the word has come to be used most commonly to describe any regime that has come to power by military overthrow of the existing governing body.

30. A tête-à-tête is French for "head to head." It means a talk or meeting.

TEST 4C ANSWERS

31. Patty Hearst, newspaper heiress and 1970s kidnap victim.

32. Perestroika, the plan for economic reform of the Soviet Union put forth by Mikhail Gorbachev.

33. Graceland, the home and final resting place of Elvis Presley, in Memphis, Tennessee.

34. *Izvestia*, Soviet newspaper.

35. The Gipper was George Gipp, Notre Dame football star.

36. Ronald Reagan played him in the movie.

37. "Papa" is the nickname by which Ernest Hemingway is remembered.

38. Dagwood Bumstead is married to Blondie.

39. E.T. stands for Extra Terrestrial.

40. Ring Lardner (1885–1933) was a famous American sports writer and short story writer.

41. Daddy Warbucks has a paternal relationship with Little Orphan Annie.

42. Dith Pran was made famous in the movie *The Killing Fields*, which chronicled his heroic struggle to escape the madness of the Pol Pot regime in Cambodia.

43. Bess Myerson, Miss America 1945, was on trial for conspiracy in 1988. Acquitted.

44. Rube Goldberg, U.S. cartoonist, is best remembered for his drawings of hopelessly complex contraptions.

45. Mel Blanc provided the voice of Bugs Bunny and a host of other cartoon characters.

46. *Couch Potato* is a term coined to describe slothful TV viewers and junk food addicts.

47. *American Gothic* is the famous painting of a dour farm couple, painted by Grant Wood (1892–1942).

48. PLO stands for the Palestine Liberation Organization.

49. Buddy Holly is best known for "Peggy Sue," but you can count yourself correct if you said "That'll Be the Day."

50. *La Prensa* is the beleaguered opposition newspaper of Nicaragua.

TEST 4D ANSWERS

51. IHS is a Greek abbreviation for the name of Jesus.

52. Charles de Gaulle (1890–1970) was once president of France, 1958–1969.

53. Black Monday, October 19, 1987, was the day the stock market lost more than 500 points.

54. A trade deficit occurs when a nation imports more goods than it exports.

55. Scotland Yard is to Great Britain as the FBI is to the United States.

56. Deng Xiaoping is the current leader of the People's Republic of China.

57. Henry Cisneros is the well-known mayor of San Antonio, Texas.

58. Crips and Bloods are youth gangs in Los Angeles.

59. Yogi Berra was a catcher for the New York Yankees and a manager for the Yankees and the New York Mets.

60. Midas fever is more commonly called gold fever.

61. An IRA is an Individual Retirement Account.

62. The IRA is the Irish Republican Army.

63. The NRA is the National Rifle Association.

64. The Fab Four were John Lennon, Paul McCartney, Ringo Starr, and George Harrison, collectively known as the Beatles, of course.

65. The escudo is the base currency of Portugal.

66. Yurts are circular dwellings.

67. *Treasure Island* was the work of Robert Louis Stevenson.

68. *Water Music* is one of the best-known musical works of George Frideric Handel (1685–1759).

69. An Edsel is an automobile and was a marketing disaster for Ford.

70. Joyce Carol Oates is a prolific American novelist.

71. A Freudian slip is an apparently accidental utterance that is said to reveal one's true feelings.

72. Oliver North was the buccaneering lieutenant colonel who was called to task during the Iran/Contra hearings.

73. The Helga Pictures were painted by Andrew Wyeth.

74. Dian Fossey worked with gorillas and was profiled in the movie *Gorillas in the Mist*.

75. "Bird" is the nickname of jazz innovator Charlie Parker.

76. Jerry Garcia is leader of The Grateful Dead, spelled "Greatful Dead" by two generations of college students.

77. *Hedda Gabler* is a play by Norwegian dramatist Henrik Ibsen (1828–1906).

78. Amnesty International is an organization concerned with human rights violations throughout the world. It seeks to publicize and redress the problems of the world's political prisoners.

79. The ACLU is the American Civil Liberties Union, a nonpartisan organization devoted to protecting the rights set forth in the U.S. Constitution.

80. *Der Meistersinger, Parsifal, Siegfried,* and *The Ring* are among the works of German composer Richard Wagner (1813–1883).

TEST 4E ANSWERS

81. The Mekong Delta is a vast, fertile delta near Ho Chi Minh City in Vietnam.

82. Kent State is the place the Ohio National Guard opened fire on a group of college students protesting the bombing of Cambodia. Four students were killed and nine wounded on May 4, 1970.

83. Wordsworthian describes attitudes toward nature associated with English romantic poet William Wordsworth (1770–1850).

84. Wilhelm Reich (1897–1957) is remembered for his work in the field of psychoanalysis and for his theory that society represses personality.

85. Eugene McCarthy was a presidential candidate in 1968, running principally on an antiwar platform.

86. Jack Ruby was the assassin of Lee Harvey Oswald, who allegedly assassinated President John Kennedy.

87. A Zionist is one who believes in the continued existence of Israel.

88. Emma Goldman (1869–1940), sometimes called "Red Emma," was a proponent of women's emancipation, an active anarchist and firebrand.

89. Art Deco was popular during the 1920s (1930s will also be accepted as a correct answer).

90. The Greenhouse Effect has it that the earth's temperature is rising due to man-made atmospheric pollution. This warming is predicted to have dire consequences.

91. Dwight Yoakam, Randy Travis, and k. d. lang are all singer/songwriters in the field of country/western music.

92. Kim Philby (1912–) was an infamous British intelligence officer who spied for the Soviets during the 1950s.

93. Tom Hayden was a student activist (in the SDS) in the 1960s, became a California state assemblyman in 1982, and married actress Jane Fonda.

94. Arthur Rimbaud (1854–1891), was a French symbolist poet. Most of his poetry was written before he was twenty years old.

95. Colorization is the practice of using computer technology to turn classic black and white movies into color. Opponents of the practice argue that it distorts the effect intended by the filmmakers.

96. Martha Graham (1894–) is a famous American dancer and choreographer.

97. H. L. Mencken (1880–1956) is remembered for his work as an American writer, editor, and critic and was noted for his scathing wit and social criticism.

98. "Shoeless" Joe Jackson, thought by many to be one of the best natural baseball players who ever played the game, was accused of taking bribes to throw the 1919 World Series.

99. Boris Pasternak *(Dr. Zhivago)* and Aleksandr Solzhenitsyn *(The Gulag Archipelago)* are both Russian writers.

100. L. L. Bean is the name of the famous catalog that markets goods for affluent outdoorspersons.

SCORING

This test is briefer than the previous two tests. Out of 100 questions, the comfort zone is 70 or more correct. A score of less than 70 correct would suggest that reading a newspaper is not an entirely rewarding experience for you. The interesting thing about regular reading, however, is that the *process* of doing it corrects the *problems* of doing it. In other words, the more you read, the more likely it is that a wider range of references and allusions will become familiar.

71–100: You are extremely well informed and broadly knowledgeable. The act of reading must be a pleasurable and rewarding experience.

51–70: You know a great deal, but you are sometimes confused or threatened by what you read. This most likely leads you to flip past certain stories and articles and bypass entire sections of the paper.

31–50: Judging by your score, it is likely that you don't find reading newspapers to be a particularly rewarding experience.

30 or less: You probably need to spend more time reading. You may have to force yourself because, for a while at least, much of what you read is going to be somewhat befuddling.

CHAPTER FIVE

BLANK LOOKS

One of our most common responses to the frustration of faulty memory is "I remember the face, but can't recall the name." This chapter is going to put that response to the test. While you might have done quite well recalling the names of famous people and events, this chapter will test how well you can associate names with faces. Our culture is decorated with visual iconography. Pictures of famous people and historic events are imprinted in our memories. We've seen the pictures everywhere: on television, in our textbooks, reprinted in magazines and newspapers. Sometimes, however, we take for granted that everyone knows who or what these pictures depict. In the case of teachers, that faulty assumption can ensure that what students don't know remains unexplained. This test is made up of twenty-five famous visual artifacts. Each picture is familiar, but do you know who or what is depicted? Let's find out.

TEST 5
BLANK LOOKS:
Picture Identification

PICTURE 1

1. Who is this? _____

2. When did he live, within a decade or two? _____

3. What was his occupation? _____

4. What is he best remembered for? _____

PICTURE 2

IDENTIFY THE THREE MEN IN THE FOREGROUND OF THIS PICTURE FROM LEFT TO RIGHT.

5. _____

6. _____

7. _____

8. They met for two historic conferences. Name one. _____

PICTURE 3

9. Who is this? _____

10. What tribe did he lead? _____

11. Where did they stage their resistance? _____

12. Where were they transported after their surrender? _____

PICTURE 4

13. Who is this? _____

14. What was his nationality? _____

15. What ironic disability afflicted him? _____

16. What is his first name? _____

PICTURE 5

17. Who is this? _____

18. How did he meet his end? _____

19. What great historical event did he help precipitate? _____

_____

20. What raid did he lead? _____

PICTURE 6

21. Who is this? _____

22. Why is he remembered? _____

23. During the Civil War, what did he serve as? _____

_____

24. What is his most famous work? _____

PICTURE 7

25. Who is this? _____

26. What was the name of his famous horse? _____

27. He suffered his greatest defeat at the battle of _____

_____

28. After the war, near the end of his life, he served as _____

_____

PICTURE 8

29. What famous historical event is depicted in this

engraving? _____

30. Name one of the two men who drafted the document

being signed. _____

31. Who was the other one? _____

32. In what year did this event take place? _____

PICTURE 9

33. Who is this? _____

34. "The Raj" was a term used to define what? _____

_____

35. Who was she married to? _____

36. Name one of her more famous prime ministers. _____

_____

PICTURE 10

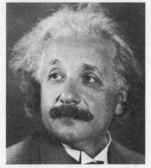

37. Who is this? _____

38. He was a genius in what field? _____

39. What equation is he commonly remembered for? _____

40. That equation led to the invention of what major weapon?

_____

PICTURE 11

41. Who is this? _____

42. Who killed him? _____

43. In what state did he die? _____

44. How old was he at his death? _____

PICTURE 12

45. Where was this? _____

46. During what war did it occur? _____

47. One of the figures was an American Indian. What is his

name? _____

48. Name the two contending forces. _____

PICTURE 13

49. Who is this? _____

50. He championed the forerunner of the United Nations.

What was it called? _____

51. When he was disabled by illness, who largely assumed his

duties? _____

52. The poster calls on people to help him. Help him with

what? _____

PICTURE 14

53. Who is the man on the left? _____

54. Who is the man in the middle? _____

55. Who is the man on the right? _____

56. Collectively, the powers they led were known as what

forces? _____

PICTURE 15

57. Who is this? _____

58. Who was the most famous playwright of her era? _____

_____

59. What is that era known as? _____

60. Who was her father? _____

PICTURE 16

61. Who is this? _____

62. Where and how did he meet his end? _____

_____

63. What work won him a Pulitzer Prize in 1953? _____

64. He was known as an afficionado of what sport? _____

PICTURE 17

65. Who is this? _____

66. She was a pioneer as what? _____

67. She disappeared during which decade of this century? ____

_____

68. At the time of her disappearance, what was she

attempting to do? _____

PICTURE 18

69. Who is this? _____

70. The year of his birth and the year of his death both

coincided with the celestial appearance of what? _____

71. What village was his boyhood home? _____

72. He gained his first national acclaim with what story?

_____

PICTURE 19

73. What is this? _____

74. In what state is it located? _____

75. Name the men sculpted on the rock from left to right.

_____

_____

76. It was the work of a sculptor and his son. Who was that

sculptor? _____

PICTURE 20

77. Who is this? _____

78. He was famous and influential during what period? _____

_____

79. What were he and others who shared his beliefs known

as? _____

80. He was born to the "peculiar institution" known as

what? _____

PICTURE 21

81. Who is this? _____

82. What was her maiden name? _____

83. What are the names of her two children? _____

_____

84. What was her second husband's nationality? _____

PICTURE 22

85. Who is this? _____

86. Where did he come from? _____

87. Where did he meet his final defeat? _____

88. On what two islands did he endure exile? _____

PICTURE 23

89. Who is this? _____

90. Who published his memoirs? _____

91. Who was his commander-in-chief? _____

92. Two famous scandals brought down his administration.

Name one. _____

PICTURE 24

93. By what name is this person best remembered? _____

_____

94. What was her real name? _____

95. She is often linked with a famous gunman. Name him.

_____

96. She is buried next to him. In what city and what state?

_____

PICTURE 25

97. Who took this famous picture? _____

98. It depicts the suffering of migrant workers during what period in our country's history? _____

99. That period was chronicled in which John Steinbeck novel? _____

100. The pictures were taken when the photographer worked for the WPA. What does WPA stand for? _____

TEST 5 ANSWERS

PICTURE 1: 1. Thomas Edison   2. 1847–1931   3. American inventor   4. The electric light and the phonograph

PICTURE 2: 5. Winston Churchill (1874–1965)   6. Franklin Roosevelt (1882–1945)   7. Josef Stalin (1879–1953)   8. Yalta or Teheran

PICTURE 3: 9. Geronimo (1829–1909)   10. Chiricahua Apaches   11. Arizona   12. Florida

PICTURE 4: 13. Beethoven (1770–1827)   14. German 15. Deafness   16. Ludwig

PICTURE 5: 17. John Brown (1800–1859)   18. He was hanged for treason   19. The Civil War   20. A raid on the government arsenal at Harper's Ferry

PICTURE 6: 21. Walt Whitman (1819–1892)   22. He is a major American poet   23. A hospital nurse in Washington, D.C.   24. *Leaves of Grass*

PICTURE 7: 25. Robert E. Lee (1807–1870)   26. Traveler 27. Gettysburg   28. President of Washington College, now Washington and Lee University

PICTURE 8: 29. The signing of the Declaration of Independence   30. Thomas Jefferson [answers in 30 and 31 can be reversed]   31. Benjamin Franklin   32. 1776

PICTURE 9: 33. Queen Victoria (1819–1901)   34. British rule in India   35. Prince Albert   36. Lord Melbourne, Lord Palmerston, Benjamin Disraeli, William Gladstone

PICTURE 10: 37. Albert Einstein (1879–1955)   38. Physics 39. $E=MC^2$ 40. The atomic bomb

PICTURE 11: 41. William Bonney, better known as Billy the Kid (1859?–1881)   42. Pat Garrett   43. New Mexico   44. 21

PICTURE 12: 45. Iwo Jima   46. World War II   47. Ira Hayes   48. Americans and Japanese

PICTURE 13: 49. Woodrow Wilson (1856–1924)   50. The League of Nations   51. His wife, Edith   52. Win the war against Germany, World War I

PICTURE 14: 53. Benito Mussolini (1883–1945)   54. Isoroku Yamamoto (1884–1943)   55. Adolf Hitler (1889–1945) 56. The Axis forces

PICTURE 15: 57. Queen Elizabeth I (1533–1603) 58. William Shakespeare   59. The Elizabethan period, or high Renaissance   60. Henry VIII

PICTURE 16: 61. Ernest Hemingway (1899–1961)   62. He committed suicide while living in Idaho   63. *The Old Man and the Sea*   64. Bullfighting

PICTURE 17: 65. Amelia Earhart (1897–1937)   66. An aviatrix   67. 1930s   68. Fly around the world

PICTURE 18: 69. Samuel Clemens, better known as Mark Twain (1835–1910)   70. Halley's Comet   71. Hannibal, Missouri   72. "The Celebrated Jumping Frog of Calaveras County"

PICTURE 19: 73. Mt. Rushmore   74. South Dakota 75. Washington, Jefferson, Teddy Roosevelt, Lincoln 76. Gutzon Borglum

PICTURE 20: 77. Frederick Douglass (1817–1895)   78. The Civil War and the years preceding and following it 79. Abolitionists   80. Slavery

PICTURE 21: 81. Jacqueline Onassis (1929–)   82. Bouvier 83. Caroline and John   84. Greek

PICTURE 22: 85. Napoleon Bonaparte (1769–1821) 86. Corsica   87. Waterloo in Belgium   88. Elba and Saint Helena

PICTURE 23: 89. Ulysses S. Grant (1822–1885)   90. Mark Twain   91. Abraham Lincoln   92. Whiskey Ring and Credit Mobilier

PICTURE 24: 93. Calamity Jane, c.1852–1903   94. Martha Jane Cannary   95. James Butler "Wild Bill" Hickok 96. Deadwood, South Dakota

PICTURE 25: 97. Dorothea Lange (1895–1965)   98. The Great Depression   99. *The Grapes of Wrath*   100. Works Project Administration

SCORING

No matter how you scored on this test, I know that nearly all of the pictures were familiar to you. If you couldn't put names and a few details together with the pictures, that's an understandable failing. However, if you drew a blank on the faces, if most of them were unfamiliar to you, then you may need to pay more attention to your world, since these are familiar cultural icons. For this test, I'm going to use standard academic scoring.

91–100: You get an A.
81–90: You get a B.
71–80: You get a C. This is about average recognition.
61–70: Alas, a D. Below average, although it is certain that a great many people did far worse.
60 or less: Failing, unfortunately. The failure is that there is much you will see in print and on TV that will not resonate for you. The solution is to pay more attention, ask questions, read.

CHAPTER SIX

AS TIME GOES BY

"It's a curse to live in interesting times," according to an old Chinese proverb. Nobody in the twentieth century has avoided that curse. Decades take on their identity and their character according to the interesting events—and there have been lots of interesting events in this century. It may be an arbitrary way of thinking about the press of history, but when we think of a particular decade, certain cultural and historical icons come automatically to mind.

Flaubert, the great French novelist, is thought to have said that "God is in the details." History, when it regains life, is in the details as well. The details, even the minutiae, revivify times gone by. That is probably why film directors pay so much attention to details when making period movies, and also why viewers begin to withhold credibility and involvement when a writer or filmmaker gets the details wrong. That is also why the more distant history tends to be somewhat less engaging; more of the details that particularize and humanize the events have been lost.

The test that follows is about the details surrounding the most significant events of this rapidly closing century. For some younger test takers, this is going to be exceedingly difficult. The way history is most often taught in schools, the most current periods (say the last fifty or sixty years) are often not covered because the course runs out before the more recent material is reached. Also, standard history courses tend to cover politics and international relations while scanting the other events that make up the story of our species on this planet. Perhaps the way history is taught should be rethought; that instead of beginning in the distant past and marching through time chronologically, history should be taught from the present backwards so that students can begin to pick up the threads and weave them back through the past. Currently, we are graduating students from high school who may be able to tell who discovered America (in the standard Christopher Columbus version) but who have never heard of the Cuban Missile Crisis, the Holocaust, or the McCarthy hearings. To me, it seems dangerous to have so much of that significant recent history lost to students. As polls and news stories report the spread of racism on American college campuses, we may be seeing indications of the price we pay when the recent past is overlooked.

But we'll put such seriousness aside for now as the test of the century looms ahead. Here are two hundred questions about typifying events, manias, styles, or labels that have become identifying symbols for various decades of this century. Your task is to pinpoint the decade in which the items originated or to which they are most commonly linked. In the case of some questions, the decade line is somewhat blurred. The answers section will accommodate answers that cross that blurry line.

TEST 6
THE TWENTIETH CENTURY DECADE BY DECADE

IDENTIFY THE FOLLOWING FADS, FOIBLES, FLARE-UPS AND FASHIONS ACCORDING TO THE DECADE WITH WHICH THEY ARE ASSOCIATED. CIRCLE THE DECADE.

1. Davy Crockett caps . . . . . 1900–10 Teens 20s 30s 40s 50s 60s 70s 80s

2. Bathtub gin . . . . 1900–10 Teens 20s 30s 40s 50s 60s 70s 80s

3. Urban cowboys . . . . 1900–10 Teens 20s 30s 40s 50s 60s 70s 80s

4. Lounge lizards . . . . 1900–10 Teens 20s 30s 40s 50s 60s 70s 80s

5. The Lost Generation . . . . 1900–10 Teens 20s 30s 40s 50s 60s 70s 80s

6. The Beat Generation . . . . 1900–10 Teens 20s 30s 40s 50s 60s 70s 80s

7. The Me Generation . . . . . 1900–10 Teens 20s 30s 40s 50s 60s 70s 80s

8. The generation gap. . . . . . 1900–10 Teens 20s 30s 40s 50s 60s 70s 80s

9. Nouvelle cuisine . . . . 1900–10 Teens 20s 30s 40s 50s 60s 70s 80s

10. The Miniskirt . . . . 1900–10 Teens 20s 30s 40s 50s 60s 70s 80s

11. The Charleston . . . . 1900–10 Teens 20s 30s 40s 50s 60s 70s 80s

12. The Twist . . . . 1900–10 Teens 20s 30s 40s 50s 60s 70s 80s

13. The Stroll . . . . 1900–10 Teens 20s 30s 40s 50s 60s 70s 80s

14. The Cakewalk . . . . 1900–10 Teens 20s 30s 40s 50s 60s 70s 80s

15. The Frug . . . . 1900–10 Teens 20s 30s 40s 50s 60s 70s 80s

16. The Turkey Trot. . . . . . . 1900–10 Teens 20s 30s 40s 50s 60s 70s 80s

17. The Jitterbug . . . . 1900–10 Teens 20s 30s 40s 50s 60s 70s 80s

18. The Checkers speech . . . 1900–10 Teens 20s 30s 40s 50s 60s 70s 80s

19. Do-it-yourself craze . . . . 1900–10 Teens 20s 30s 40s 50s 60s 70s 80s

20. Fitness craze . . . . 1900–10 Teens 20s 30s 40s 50s 60s 70s 80s

21. Sideburns/ducktail . . . . . 1900–10 Teens 20s 30s 40s 50s 60s 70s 80s

22. Bra burning . . . . 1900–10 Teens 20s 30s 40s 50s 60s 70s 80s

23. Draft card burning . . . . . 1900–10 Teens 20s 30s 40s 50s 60s 70s 80s

24. Gold Star Mothers . . . . . 1900–10 Teens 20s 30s 40s 50s 60s 70s 80s

25. St. Valentine's Day
Massacre . . . . 1900–10 Teens 20s 30s 40s 50s 60s 70s 80s

26. Freedom Riders . . . . 1900–10 Teens 20s 30s 40s 50s 60s 70s 80s

27. Rudolph Valentino . . . . . 1900–10 Teens 20s 30s 40s 50s 60s 70s 80s

28. Army/McCarthy
hearings . . . . 1900–10 Teens 20s 30s 40s 50s 60s 70s 80s

29. Watergate hearings . . . . . 1900–10 Teens 20s 30s 40s 50s 60s 70s 80s

30. The Scopes Trial . . . . . . 1900–10 Teens 20s 30s 40s 50s 60s 70s 80s

31. Manhattan Project . . . . . 1900–10 Teens 20s 30s 40s 50s 60s 70s 80s

32. The rise of Levittown . . . 1900–10 Teens 20s 30s 40s 50s 60s 70s 80s

33. *The Feminine Mystique* . 1900–10 Teens 20s 30s 40s 50s 60s 70s 80s

34. Hot Jazz . . . . 1900–10 Teens 20s 30s 40s 50s 60s 70s 80s

35. Cool Jazz . . . . 1900–10 Teens 20s 30s 40s 50s 60s 70s 80s

36. *Rock Around the Clock* . 1900–10 Teens 20s 30s 40s 50s 60s 70s 80s

37. Be-bop . . . . 1900–10 Teens 20s 30s 40s 50s 60s 70s 80s

38. Swing bands . . . . 1900–10 Teens 20s 30s 40s 50s 60s 70s 80s

39. Rudy Vallee . . . . 1900–10 Teens 20s 30s 40s 50s 60s 70s 80s

40. The G.I. Bill . . . . 1900–10 Teens 20s 30s 40s 50s 60s 70s 80s

41. Backyard fallout shelters . 1900–10 Teens 20s 30s 40s 50s 60s 70s 80s

42. Rosie the Riveter . . . . . . 1900–10 Teens 20s 30s 40s 50s 60s 70s 80s

43. "Over There" . . . . 1900–10 Teens 20s 30s 40s 50s 60s 70s 80s

44. The Volstead Act . . . . . . 1900–10 Teens 20s 30s 40s 50s 60s 70s 80s

45. 3-D glasses/movies . . . . . 1900–10 Teens 20s 30s 40s 50s 60s 70s 80s

46. Flower children . . . . 1900–10 Teens 20s 30s 40s 50s 60s 70s 80s

47. L.A. Gear . . . . 1900–10 Teens 20s 30s 40s 50s 60s 70s 80s

48. The Bull Moose Party . . . 1900–10 Teens 20s 30s 40s 50s 60s 70s 80s

49. LSD . . . . 1900–10 Teens 20s 30s 40s 50s 60s 70s 80s

50. Crack . . . . 1900–10 Teens 20s 30s 40s 50s 60s 70s 80s

51. Talkies . . . . 1900–10 Teens 20s 30s 40s 50s 60s 70s 80s

52. TV dinners . . . . 1900–10 Teens 20s 30s 40s 50s 60s 70s 80s

53. The Free Speech
Movement . . . . 1900–10 Teens 20s 30s 40s 50s 60s 70s 80s

54. Rubik's Cube . . . . 1900–10 Teens 20s 30s 40s 50s 60s 70s 80s

55. Uncle Miltie . . . . 1900–10 Teens 20s 30s 40s 50s 60s 70s 80s

56. The bikini . . . . 1900–10 Teens 20s 30s 40s 50s 60s 70s 80s

57. The topless . . . . 1900–10 Teens 20s 30s 40s 50s 60s 70s 80s

58. Spandex . . . . 1900–10 Teens 20s 30s 40s 50s 60s 70s 80s

59. White bucks . . . . 1900–10 Teens 20s 30s 40s 50s 60s 70s 80s

60. Raccoon coats . . . . 1900–10 Teens 20s 30s 40s 50s 60s 70s 80s

61. "Wrong Way" Corrigan . . 1900–10 Teens 20s 30s 40s 50s 60s 70s 80s

62. The Great Influenza
Epidemic . . . . 1900–10 Teens 20s 30s 40s 50s 60s 70s 80s

63. Swine flu . . . . 1900–10 Teens 20s 30s 40s 50s 60s 70s 80s

64. Polio vaccine . . . . 1900–10 Teens 20s 30s 40s 50s 60s 70s 80s

65. AIDS . . . . 1900–10 Teens 20s 30s 40s 50s 60s 70s 80s

66. Heart transplants . . . . . . 1900–10 Teens 20s 30s 40s 50s 60s 70s 80s

67. The WPA . . . . 1900–10 Teens 20s 30s 40s 50s 60s 70s 80s

68. *The Grapes of Wrath* . . . 1900–10 Teens 20s 30s 40s 50s 60s 70s 80s

69. The Civil Rights Act . . . 1900–10 Teens 20s 30s 40s 50s 60s 70s 80s

70. The ERA . . . . 1900–10 Teens 20s 30s 40s 50s 60s 70s 80s

71. Social Security . . . . 1900–10 Teens 20s 30s 40s 50s 60s 70s 80s

72. The Fatty Arbuckle
Scandal . . . . 1900–10 Teens 20s 30s 40s 50s 60s 70s 80s

73. OKIES . . . . 1900–10 Teens 20s 30s 40s 50s 60s 70s 80s

74. The Homeless . . . . 1900–10 Teens 20s 30s 40s 50s 60s 70s 80s

75. Boat People . . . . 1900–10 Teens 20s 30s 40s 50s 60s 70s 80s

76. First U.S. child labor
laws . . . . 1900–10 Teens 20s 30s 40s 50s 60s 70s 80s

77. "Loose lips sink ships" . . 1900–10 Teens 20s 30s 40s 50s 60s 70s 80s

78. Ragtime . . . . 1900–10 Teens 20s 30s 40s 50s 60s 70s 80s

79. The Back-to-Africa
Movement . . . . 1900–10 Teens 20s 30s 40s 50s 60s 70s 80s

80. Hi-fi . . . . 1900–10 Teens 20s 30s 40s 50s 60s 70s 80s

81. Compact discs . . . . 1900–10 Teens 20s 30s 40s 50s 60s 70s 80s

82. Harlem Renaissance . . . . 1900–10 Teens 20s 30s 40s 50s 60s 70s 80s

83. Pop Art . . . . 1900–10 Teens 20s 30s 40s 50s 60s 70s 80s

84. Art Deco . . . . 1900–10 Teens 20s 30s 40s 50s 60s 70s 80s

85. Cubism . . . . 1900–10 Teens 20s 30s 40s 50s 60s 70s 80s

86. Dadaism . . . . 1900–10 Teens 20s 30s 40s 50s 60s 70s 80s

87. Surrealism . . . . 1900–10 Teens 20s 30s 40s 50s 60s 70s 80s

88. Televangelism . . . . 1900–10 Teens 20s 30s 40s 50s 60s 70s 80s

89. Mouseketeers . . . . 1900–10 Teens 20s 30s 40s 50s 60s 70s 80s

90. *Sesame Street* . . . . 1900–10 Teens 20s 30s 40s 50s 60s 70s 80s

91. *Father Knows Best* . . . . . 1900–10 Teens 20s 30s 40s 50s 60s 70s 80s

92. Altamont . . . . 1900–10 Teens 20s 30s 40s 50s 60s 70s 80s

93. The Singing Cowboys . . . 1900–10 Teens 20s 30s 40s 50s 60s 70s 80s

94. The Profumo Affair . . . . 1900–10 Teens 20s 30s 40s 50s 60s 70s 80s

95. The Falklands War . . . . . 1900–10 Teens 20s 30s 40s 50s 60s 70s 80s

96. Invasion of Grenada . . . . 1900–10 Teens 20s 30s 40s 50s 60s 70s 80s

97. Big Band Era . . . . 1900–10 Teens 20s 30s 40s 50s 60s 70s 80s

98. Aimee Semple
McPherson . . . . 1900–10 Teens 20s 30s 40s 50s 60s 70s 80s

99. *Playboy* . . . . 1900–10 Teens 20s 30s 40s 50s 60s 70s 80s

100. Keystone Cops . . . . 1900–10 Teens 20s 30s 40s 50s 60s 70s 80s

101. Saturday serials . . . . . . 1900–10 Teens 20s 30s 40s 50s 60s 70s 80s

102. *Friday Night Fights* . . . 1900–10 Teens 20s 30s 40s 50s 60s 70s 80s

103. Nehru jackets . . . . 1900–10 Teens 20s 30s 40s 50s 60s 70s 80s

104. Circle skirts . . . . 1900–10 Teens 20s 30s 40s 50s 60s 70s 80s

105. The chemise . . . . 1900–10 Teens 20s 30s 40s 50s 60s 70s 80s

106. The tent dress . . . . 1900–10 Teens 20s 30s 40s 50s 60s 70s 80s

107. Discos . . . . 1900–10 Teens 20s 30s 40s 50s 60s 70s 80s

108. Speakeasies . . . . 1900–10 Teens 20s 30s 40s 50s 60s 70s 80s

109. Peter Max . . . . 1900–10 Teens 20s 30s 40s 50s 60s 70s 80s

110. Barbie dolls . . . . 1900–10 Teens 20s 30s 40s 50s 60s 70s 80s

111. *American Bandstand* . . 1900–10 Teens 20s 30s 40s 50s 60s 70s 80s

112. *Mayaguez* Incident . . . . 1900–10 Teens 20s 30s 40s 50s 60s 70s 80s

113. The U-2 Incident . . . . . 1900–10 Teens 20s 30s 40s 50s 60s 70s 80s

114. The Bonus Army . . . . . 1900–10 Teens 20s 30s 40s 50s 60s 70s 80s

115. The teddy bear . . . . 1900–10 Teens 20s 30s 40s 50s 60s 70s 80s

116. "Sick" Comedians . . . . 1900–10 Teens 20s 30s 40s 50s 60s 70s 80s

117. The Bicentennial . . . . . 1900–10 Teens 20s 30s 40s 50s 60s 70s 80s

118. Brainwashing . . . . 1900–10 Teens 20s 30s 40s 50s 60s 70s 80s

119. Bridey Murphy . . . . 1900–10 Teens 20s 30s 40s 50s 60s 70s 80s

120. Japanese internment
camps. . . . . 1900–10 Teens 20s 30s 40s 50s 60s 70s 80s

121. John Dillinger . . . . 1900–10 Teens 20s 30s 40s 50s 60s 70s 80s

122. Flappers. . . . . 1900–10 Teens 20s 30s 40s 50s 60s 70s 80s

123. The Black Panthers. . . . 1900–10 Teens 20s 30s 40s 50s 60s 70s 80s

124. Ration stamps . . . . 1900–10 Teens 20s 30s 40s 50s 60s 70s 80s

125. VCRs. . . . . 1900–10 Teens 20s 30s 40s 50s 60s 70s 80s

126. The PTL . . . . 1900–10 Teens 20s 30s 40s 50s 60s 70s 80s

127. *Catcher in the Rye* . . . . 1900–10 Teens 20s 30s 40s 50s 60s 70s 80s

128. *Lord of the Flies* . . . . . . 1900–10 Teens 20s 30s 40s 50s 60s 70s 80s

129. The Watts Riot. . . . . . . 1900–10 Teens 20s 30s 40s 50s 60s 70s 80s

130. Hula Hoop. . . . . 1900–10 Teens 20s 30s 40s 50s 60s 70s 80s

131. The space shuttle . . . . . 1900–10 Teens 20s 30s 40s 50s 60s 70s 80s

132. TVA/rural
electrification . . . . 1900–10 Teens 20s 30s 40s 50s 60s 70s 80s

133. Debbie and Eddie . . . . . 1900–10 Teens 20s 30s 40s 50s 60s 70s 80s

134. Lend-lease . . . . 1900–10 Teens 20s 30s 40s 50s 60s 70s 80s

135. The 26 July Movement/
Overthrow of Batista . . . . . . 1900–10 Teens 20s 30s 40s 50s 60s 70s 80s

136. Wife swapping . . . . 1900–10 Teens 20s 30s 40s 50s 60s 70s 80s

137. Victory gardens . . . . . . 1900–10 Teens 20s 30s 40s 50s 60s 70s 80s

138. Encounter groups . . . . . 1900–10 Teens 20s 30s 40s 50s 60s 70s 80s

139. The Warsaw Alliance . . 1900–10 Teens 20s 30s 40s 50s 60s 70s 80s

140. The United Nations . . . 1900–10 Teens 20s 30s 40s 50s 60s 70s 80s

141. *Forever Amber* . . . . 1900–10 Teens 20s 30s 40s 50s 60s 70s 80s

142. *The Valley of the Dolls* . 1900–10 Teens 20s 30s 40s 50s 60s 70s 80s

143. "We will bury you". . . . 1900–10 Teens 20s 30s 40s 50s 60s 70s 80s

144. V-Mail. . . . . 1900–10 Teens 20s 30s 40s 50s 60s 70s 80s

145. Porkchop Hill. . . . . 1900–10 Teens 20s 30s 40s 50s 60s 70s 80s

146. Paper drives . . . . 1900–10 Teens 20s 30s 40s 50s 60s 70s 80s

147. The Munich Olympics . 1900–10 Teens 20s 30s 40s 50s 60s 70s 80s

148. The Dustbowl . . . . 1900–10 Teens 20s 30s 40s 50s 60s 70s 80s

149. The *Titanic* . . . . 1900–10 Teens 20s 30s 40s 50s 60s 70s 80s

150. The Wright Brothers . . . 1900–10 Teens 20s 30s 40s 50s 60s 70s 80s

151. The *Hindenburg*. . . . . . 1900–10 Teens 20s 30s 40s 50s 60s 70s 80s

152. *The $64,000 Question*. . 1900–10 Teens 20s 30s 40s 50s 60s 70s 80s

153. Vanna White . . . . 1900–10 Teens 20s 30s 40s 50s 60s 70s 80s

154. Betty Grable . . . . 1900–10 Teens 20s 30s 40s 50s 60s 70s 80s

155. Mary Pickford . . . . 1900–10 Teens 20s 30s 40s 50s 60s 70s 80s

156. Brigitte Bardot . . . . 1900–10 Teens 20s 30s 40s 50s 60s 70s 80s

157. Shirley Temple . . . . 1900–10 Teens 20s 30s 40s 50s 60s 70s 80s

158. Nickelodeons . . . . 1900–10 Teens 20s 30s 40s 50s 60s 70s 80s

159. Payola . . . . 1900–10 Teens 20s 30s 40s 50s 60s 70s 80s

160. Irangate . . . . 1900–10 Teens 20s 30s 40s 50s 60s 70s 80s

161. "Lucky Strike Green
has gone to war" . . . . 1900–10 Teens 20s 30s 40s 50s 60s 70s 80s

162. SDS. . . . . 1900–10 Teens 20s 30s 40s 50s 60s 70s 80s

163. The Brat Pack. . . . . 1900–10 Teens 20s 30s 40s 50s 60s 70s 80s

164. The Rat Pack . . . . 1900–10 Teens 20s 30s 40s 50s 60s 70s 80s

165. Bobby soxers . . . . 1900–10 Teens 20s 30s 40s 50s 60s 70s 80s

166. Lindbergh kidnapping . . 1900–10 Teens 20s 30s 40s 50s 60s 70s 80s

167. Heartbreak Ridge . . . . . 1900–10 Teens 20s 30s 40s 50s 60s 70s 80s

168. The Tet Offensive . . . . . 1900–10 Teens 20s 30s 40s 50s 60s 70s 80s

169. Omaha Beach. . . . . 1900–10 Teens 20s 30s 40s 50s 60s 70s 80s

170. Nineteenth
Amendment . . . . 1900–10 Teens 20s 30s 40s 50s 60s 70s 80s

171. Bobbed hair . . . . 1900–10 Teens 20s 30s 40s 50s 60s 70s 80s

172. "Mademoiselles from
Armentières" . . . . 1900–10 Teens 20s 30s 40s 50s 60s 70s 80s

173. "I'll Be Seeing You". . . . 1900–10 Teens 20s 30s 40s 50s 60s 70s 80s

174. "Light My Fire" . . . . . . 1900–10 Teens 20s 30s 40s 50s 60s 70s 80s

175. "It's a Long Way to
Tipperary" . . . . 1900–10 Teens 20s 30s 40s 50s 60s 70s 80s

176. "How Much Is That
Doggy in the Window?" . . . . 1900–10 Teens 20s 30s 40s 50s 60s 70s 80s

177. The *Lusitania* . . . . 1900–10 Teens 20s 30s 40s 50s 60s 70s 80s

178. Joe Louis KOs Max
Schmeling . . . . 1900–10 Teens 20s 30s 40s 50s 60s 70s 80s

179. Jessie Owens victorious
at Berlin Olympics . . . . 1900–10 Teens 20s 30s 40s 50s 60s 70s 80s

180. Cabbage Patch Dolls . . . 1900–10 Teens 20s 30s 40s 50s 60s 70s 80s

181. The Suez Crisis . . . . . . 1900–10 Teens 20s 30s 40s 50s 60s 70s 80s

182. India independence . . . . 1900–10 Teens 20s 30s 40s 50s 60s 70s 80s

183. The Great Society . . . . 1900–10 Teens 20s 30s 40s 50s 60s 70s 80s

184. The New Deal . . . . 1900–10 Teens 20s 30s 40s 50s 60s 70s 80s

185. The New Frontier . . . . . 1900–10 Teens 20s 30s 40s 50s 60s 70s 80s

186. The Bhopal disaster . . . 1900–10 Teens 20s 30s 40s 50s 60s 70s 80s

187. Rambo . . . . 1900–10 Teens 20s 30s 40s 50s 60s 70s 80s

188. The fall of Saigon . . . . . 1900–10 Teens 20s 30s 40s 50s 60s 70s 80s

189. Russian Revolution . . . . 1900–10 Teens 20s 30s 40s 50s 60s 70s 80s

190. *The Organization Man* . 1900–10 Teens 20s 30s 40s 50s 60s 70s 80s

191. The first San Francisco
Earthquake . . . . 1900–10 Teens 20s 30s 40s 50s 60s 70s 80s

192. "Brother, Can You Spare
a Dime?" . . . . 1900–10 Teens 20s 30s 40s 50s 60s 70s 80s

193. Liston/Clay fight . . . . . 1900–10 Teens 20s 30s 40s 50s 60s 70s 80s

194. Death of Allende/
Chilean coup . . . . 1900–10 Teens 20s 30s 40s 50s 60s 70s 80s

195. *Saturday Night Fever* . . 1900–10 Teens 20s 30s 40s 50s 60s 70s 80s

196. *King Kong* . . . . 1900–10 Teens 20s 30s 40s 50s 60s 70s 80s

197. Michael J. Fox . . . . 1900–10 Teens 20s 30s 40s 50s 60s 70s 80s

198. The IWW (Wobblies) . . . 1900–10 Teens 20s 30s 40s 50s 60s 70s 80s

199. Woodrow Wilson's 14
Points . . . . 1900–10 Teens 20s 30s 40s 50s 60s 70s 80s

200. Florida land boom/
bust . . . . 1900–10 Teens 20s 30s 40s 50s 60s 70s 80s

Even from this brief sampling, it is easy to see that the twentieth century has been crammed with details. "Anything worth knowing," according to Saki, "one practically teaches oneself, and the rest obtrudes itself sooner or later." If you've lived long enough, many of the details on this test have obtruded themselves into your life. Even if you're a bit younger, you have probably heard about most of these things. Check your answers to see how much you've taught yourself, or how much of the myriad fashions, foibles, and phenomena of the twentieth century has obtruded into your knowledge.

TEST 6: ANSWERS

1. Davy Crockett caps..............................1950s
2. Bathtub gin 1920s
3. Urban cowboys 1970s
4. Lounge lizards 1920s
5. The Lost Generation 1920s
6. The Beat Generation 1950s
7. The Me Generation 1970s
8. The generation gap 1960s
9. Nouvelle cuisine 1970s
10. The Miniskirt 1960s
11. The Charleston 1920s
12. The Twist...................................1960s
13. The Stroll..................................1950s
14. The Cakewalk..............................1900–10
15. The Frug 1960s
16. The Turkey Trot.............................Teens
17. The Jitterbug 1940s
18. The Checkers speech 1950s
19. Do-it-yourself craze........................1950s
20. Fitness craze 1980s
21. Sideburns/ducktail 1950s
22. Bra burning 1970s
23. Draft card burning 1960s
24. Gold Star Mothers...........................1940s
25. St. Valentine's Day Massacre 1920s
26. Freedom Riders 1960s
27. Rudolph Valentino...........................1920s

28. Army/McCarthy hearings 1950s
29. Watergate hearings 1970s
30. The Scopes Trial 1920s
31. Manhattan Project. 1940s
32. The rise of Levittown 1940s
33. *The Feminine Mystique* 1960s
34. Hot jazz 1920s
35. Cool jazz 1950s
36. *Rock Around the Clock* 1950s
37. Be-bop. 1940s
38. Swing bands. 1930s
39. Rudy Vallee 1920s
40. The G.I. Bill. 1940s
41. Backyard fallout shelters 1950s
42. Rosie the Riveter. 1940s
43. "Over There" . . . . Teens
44. The Volstead Act . . . . Teens
45. 3-D glasses/movies 1950s
46. Flower children 1960s
47. L.A. Gear 1980s
48. The Bull Moose Party . . . . Teens
49. LSD 1960s
50. Crack 1980s
51. Talkies 1920s
52. TV dinners. 1950s
53. The Free Speech Movement. 1960s
54. Rubik's Cube 1970s
55. Uncle Miltie 1950s
56. The bikini 1950s
57. The topless 1960s

148. The Dustbowl 1930s

149. The *Titanic* . . . . Teens

150. The Wright Brothers. 1900–10

151. The *Hindenburg* 1930s

152. *The $64,000 Question* 1950s

153. Vanna White 1980s

154. Betty Grable 1940s

155. Mary Pickford 1920s

156. Brigitte Bardot 1950s

157. Shirley Temple. 1930s

158. Nickelodeons 1900–10

159. Payola. 1950s

160. Irangate 1980s

161. "Lucky Strike Green has gone to war" 1940s

162. SDS. 1960s

163. The Brat Pack 1980s

164. The Rat Pack 1960s

165. Bobby soxers 1940s

166. Lindbergh kidnapping. 1930s

167. Heartbreak Ridge 1950s

168. The Tet Offensive 1960s

169. Omaha Beach 1940s

170. Nineteenth Amendment. Teens

171. Bobbed hair 1920s

172. "Mademoiselles from Armentières". . . . . Teens

173. "I'll Be Seeing You" 1940s

174. "Light My Fire" 1960s

175. "It's a Long Way to Tipperary" . . . . Teens

176. "How Much Is That Doggy in the Window?" 1950s

177. The *Lusitania* . . . . Teens

178. Joe Louis KOs Max Schmeling 1930s

179. Jessie Owens victorious at Berlin Olympics 1930s

180. Cabbage Patch Dolls 1980s

181. The Suez Crisis 1950s

182. India independence 1940s

183. The Great Society 1960s

184. The New Deal 1930s

185. The New Frontier 1960s

186. The Bhopal disaster 1980s

187. Rambo 1980s

188. The fall of Saigon 1970s

189. Russian Revolution . . . . Teens

190. *The Organization Man* 1950s

191. The first San Francisco Earthquake 1900–10

192. "Brother, Can You Spare a Dime?" 1930s

193. Liston/Clay fight 1960s

194. Death of Allende/overthrow of Chile 1970s

195. *Saturday Night Fever* 1970s

196. *King Kong* 1930s

197. Michael J. Fox 1980s

198. The IWW (Wobblies) 1900–10

199. Woodrow Wilson's 14 Points . . . . Teens

200. Florida land boom/bust 1920s

SCORING

Because younger people are somewhat handicapped in taking this test, it seems fair to make some compensatory apparatus for scoring. In assessing your score, add 20 points to your total number of correct answers if you're under twenty years old. Add 10 points to your total if you're under thirty years old. If you're under forty years old, add 5 points to your total. Over forty and you are expected to settle for your actual achieved point total.

181–200: You're a true child of your century and you know much about its characterizing events.

141–180: You've stored a great deal in your memory bank. Count yourself knowledgeable about the times leading to our times.

101–140: Only fair, but nothing to feel sheepish about. Either on the far end, or on the near end, there are things you either weren't aware of, or took little interest in.

100 or less: Much of the interesting detail of history has somehow escaped your attention. You might wish to know more about the century that welcomed you to this planet.

CHAPTER SEVEN

WHERE IN THE WORLD ARE WE?

Since the schools have largely abandoned teaching geography to elementary and secondary students, it might just be that lucrative new opportunities will be turning up for the unscrupulous in the travel agency business. Given current ignorance of the geography of the planet, dishonest travel agents could make a lot of money booking people for expensive trips far away, then sending them to nearer, cheaper places. By the evidence, few Americans would know the difference.

A *National Geographic* survey revealed that one in seven, or the equivalent of 24 million, Americans could not identify the United States on a blank map of the world. Americans fall near the bottom of the surveys when it comes to knowing where we are.

Not long ago, my sister came for a visit to our home in Washington state. One of her friends hoped she would get a chance to see the Statue of Liberty, another hoped she would get to see the Washington Monument. A teacher of geography wrote to tell me of students who routinely locate foreign countries within the continental boundaries of the United States. A student of international affairs from New Mexico writes: "We are supposed to be a world power, but we are ignorant, and here, in an international setting, our ignorance is very visible. It was an embarrassment to have classmates from countries we had not heard of. We (U.S. students) were always ending up asking the 'stupid questions' that everyone from most every country had already studied in grade school."

A teacher at a Boston community college tested her students with a blank map of the world and found that some students placed Canada in the middle of Australia or identified the

United States as Brazil, England, or India. Oceans were labeled as countries. Seventy percent of the 373 students tested could not locate England; 81 percent could not find Japan. And in a survey done in Miami, Florida, significant numbers of Miamians didn't know where Miami was.

Test 7A
WHERE IN THE WORLD WOULD YOU BE?

FOREIGNERS HAVE AN ANNOYING HABIT OF CALLING THE PLACES WHERE THEY LIVE SOMETHING OTHER THAN WHAT WE KNOW THEM BY. IT IS, I SUPPOSE, JUST ONE MORE WAY IN WHICH THE TOURIST IS KEPT BEWILDERED AND CONFUSED. NONETHELESS, SINCE THE WORLD WON'T BEND TO OUR ETHNOCENTRIC AND NATIONALISTIC VIEW OF IT, IT IS IMPORTANT TO KNOW HOW PLACES ARE KNOWN TO THE PEOPLE WHO LIVE THERE.

IF SOME FAIR MORNING YOU AWOKE WITH JET LAG TO FIND YOURSELF IN THE FOLLOWING PLACES, WHERE IN THE WORLD WOULD YOU BE?

1. München is better known to Americans as _____ and is located in _____

2. Wien is better known to Americans as _____ and is located in _____

3. Formosa is also known as _____ and is located in _____

4. Luzern is better known to Americans as _____ and is located in _____

5. Baile Átha Cliath is better known as _____ and is located in _____

6. Praha is better known in the West as _____ and is located in _____

7. Moskva is known to the English-speaking world as _____ and is located in _____

8. Lisboa is known to Americans as _____ and is located in _____

9. Kampuchea is more commonly known in America as _____

_____

10. Beograd is known to Americans as _____ and is

located in _____

11. Krung Thep is the name by which _____ is known

by its inhabitants. It's located in _____

12. Eire is the place we call _____

13. Köln is better known to Americans as _____ and

is located in _____

14. Athínai is what the _____ people call this

city. It is better known to us as _____

15. Persia is the ancient name for _____

16. Hades, an out-of-this-world "vacation" spot, is better

known as _____

17. Bucureşti is called _____ on the evening

news. It is located in _____

18. Ho Chi Minh City used to be known as _____

and is located in _____

19. Napoli is, of course, another way of saying _____,

which is located in _____. People there are

known as _____

20. Venezia is what the _____ people call _____

About five of the previous questions are obscure or difficult. The rest are likely to be easier because they are cognates of the names we know those places by. In any case, most of the questions require two or more answers. You must fill in all the blanks correctly in order to score one point per question.

Now, if you are reasonably sure you know your way around, proceed to the next set of questions. But proceed even if you are not sure. This next set may prove easier.

TEST 7B
THEY LEFT THEIR NAMES BEHIND

FROM SEA TO SEA, THE AMERICAN INDIANS LEFT THEIR NAMES ON THE LAND THAT WAS ONCE THEIRS. IN WHAT STATES ARE THE FOLLOWING CITIES AND TOWNS, ALL OF THEM NAMED BY OR FOR INDIANS?

21. Ottumwa _____

22. Winnemucca _____

23. Yakima _____

24. Tuscaloosa _____

25. Peoria _____

26. Minneapolis _____

27. Pensacola _____

28. Pocatello _____

29. Milwaukee _____

30. Ocala _____

31. Harlem is in _____ and was named by settlers from Haarlem in _____

32. Ithaca is in _____, but was named after this island off the coast of _____

MORE OFTEN THAN NOT, HOWEVER, THE ORIGINAL INDIAN NAMES FOR PLACES WERE CHANGED BY THE IMMIGRANTS, WHO FREQUENTLY NAMED THE PLACES

THEY SETTLED
AFTER THE PLACES
THEY CAME FROM.
IN THE NEXT SET OF
QUESTIONS, LOCATE
THE FOLLOWING U.S.
TOWNS AND CITIES
BY THEIR RESPECTIVE
STATES, THEN
IDENTIFY THE
COUNTRY FROM
WHICH THE NAME
CAME.

33. New Orleans is, of course, in _____, but was named in honor of the city of Orléans in _____

34. Memphis is in _____ and is named for a capital of ancient _____

35. Toledo is in _____ and shares its name with Toledo, _____

Now we'll become global once again as we look at places best remembered because of memorable events that occurred there.

TEST 7C
WHAT WENT ON HERE?

36. Waterloo is in the country of _____. It was the site of _____

37. Lourdes is in _____. It was the site of _____

38. Bethlehem is in _____. It was the site of _____

39. Gallipoli is in _____. It was the site of _____

40. Harper's Ferry is in the state of _____. It was the site of _____

41. Soweto is in _____. It is (and was) the site of _____

42. Hastings is in the country of _____.

It was the site of _____

43. Sutter's Fort is in the state of _____.

It was the site of _____

44. Gettysburg is in the state of _____. It

was the site of _____

45. Greenwich is in the country of _____.

It is the site of _____

46. The Bay of Pigs is in _____. It was

the site of _____

47. Loch Ness is in _____. It is the

site of _____

48. Donner Pass is in _____. It was the

site of _____

49. Selma is in the state of _____. It

was the site of _____

50. Tombstone is in the state of _____.

It was the site of _____

51. Auschwitz is in _____. It was

the site of _____

52. Ticonderoga is in the state of _____. It

was the site of _____

53. Guernica is in _____. It was

the site of _____

54. Chernobyl is in _____. It

was the site of _____

55. Fort Sumter is in the state of _____.

It was the site of _____

56. San Juan Hill is in _____. It

was the site of _____

57. Alcatraz is in the state of _____.

It was the site of _____

58. Woodstock is in the state of _____.

It was the site of _____

59. Corregidor is in _____. It was

the site of _____

60. Stonehenge is in _____. It

is the site of _____

61. Potsdam is in _____. It was

the site of _____

62. The Somme is in _____. It was the site of _____

63. Nagasaki is in _____. It was the site of _____

64. Runnymede is in _____. It was the site of _____

65. Pompeii is in _____. It was the site of _____

TEST 7D
WHERE DID THEY COME FROM?

SOME PLACES ARE REMEMBERED PRINCIPALLY FOR THEIR FAMOUS DAUGHTERS AND SONS. THE FOLLOWING PLACES ARE CHIEFLY REMEMBERED FOR THE FAMOUS PEOPLE WHO WERE BORN OR LIVED THERE. WHERE IN THE WORLD ARE THESE PLACES? WHO IS ASSOCIATED WITH THEM?

66. Hannibal is in the state of _____ and was the birthplace of _____

67. Amherst is in the state of _____ and is known as the home of "the belle of Amherst," _____

68. Liverpool is in _____ and was where _____ came from.

69. Elsinore is in _____ and is associated with the character of _____

70. Orléans is in _____ and is forever associated with _____

TEST 7E
RIVER DEEP, MOUNTAIN HIGH

71. Madagascar . Island_____	River_____	Mountain_____	Lake_____
72. Mindanao . . Island_____	River_____	Mountain_____	Lake_____
73. Orinoco . . . . Island_____	River_____	Mountain_____	Lake_____
74. Lassen . . . . . Island_____	River_____	Mountain_____	Lake_____
75. Titicaca . . . . Island_____	River_____	Mountain_____	Lake_____
76. Sardinia . . . . Island_____	River_____	Mountain_____	Lake_____
77. Mauna Loa . . . . Island_____	River_____	Mountain_____	Lake_____
78. Euphrates. . . Island_____	River_____	Mountain_____	Lake_____
79. Java . . . . Island_____	River_____	Mountain_____	Lake_____
80. Ararat. . . . . . Island_____	River_____	Mountain_____	Lake_____

TEST 7F
ALWAYS ON THE NEWS

81. The West Bank _____

82. Londonderry _____

83. Zimbabwe _____

84. Addis Ababa _____

85. Zurich _____

86. Helsinki _____

87. Nicosia _____

88. Beijing _____

89. Bethesda _____

90. Teheran _____

91. Phnom Penh _____

SURELY YOU KNOW THE DIFFERENCE BETWEEN A MOUNTAIN AND A RIVER, BETWEEN AN ISLAND AND A LAKE.

PERHAPS NOT.

ARE THE FOLLOWING PLACES ISLANDS, RIVERS, MOUNTAINS, OR LAKES? CHECK ONE.

THE NEXT FIFTEEN PLACES SEEM TO BE IN THE NEWS ALL THE TIME. WHERE ARE THESE PLACES?

92. East Berlin _____

93. Lesotho _____

94. Tel Aviv _____

95. The United Nations _____

TEST 7G
THE LOST PLACES

LIKE PEOPLE, PLACES SOMETIMES CHANGE THEIR NAMES. IN THE FOLLOWING LIST YOU WILL FIND NAMES OF COUNTRIES, CITIES, AND LOCALITIES THAT ARE NO LONGER KNOWN BY THOSE NAMES DUE TO CONQUEST, LIBERATION, OR CHANGE OF NATIONAL IDENTITY. THE NAMES HAVE CHANGED; THE PLACES REMAIN. WHAT ARE THE CURRENT NAMES?

96. Siam _____

97. Constantinople _____

98. Cathay _____

99. Persia _____

100. Abyssinia _____

101. Mesopotamia _____

102. Rhodesia _____

103. Seward's Folly _____

104. The Sandwich Islands _____

105. The Gadsden Purchase _____

TEST 7H
STREET SMARTS

THERE ARE FAMOUS STREETS AND BOULEVARDS IN THE WORLD THAT TURN UP IN LITERATURE, CONVERSATION, AND THE DAILY NEWS. THE FOLLOWING SECTION IS DESIGNED TO DETERMINE IF YOU KNOW WHERE THESE FAMOUS STREETS ARE. IN WHAT CITIES ARE THESE FAMOUS STREETS TO BE FOUND?

106. Savile Row _____

107. The Via Veneto _____

108. Bourbon Street _____

109. Rodeo Drive _____

110. The Autobahn _____

111. Tiananmen Square _____

112. The Ginza _____

113. Pennsylvania Avenue _____

114. The Loop _____

115. Wall Street _____

TEST 71
RIVERS OF MEMORY

SUPPOSE, AS IN SOME BAD MOVIE, YOU AWOKE TO FIND YOURSELF FLOATING DOWN A RIVER. YOU ARE BEWILDERED AND CALL TO SOMEONE ON SHORE. THE NAME IS CALLED BACK TO YOU. WOULD THAT HELP YOU TO KNOW WHERE YOU WERE? TAKE THIS TEST OF SOME OF THE MAJOR RIVERS OF THE WORLD AND FIND OUT HOW ADAPTABLE YOU MIGHT BE IF EVER YOUR BAD DREAMS COME TRUE.

IF YOU FOUND YOURSELF AFLOAT ON ANY OF THE FOLLOWING RIVERS, WHAT COUNTRY WOULD YOU BE IN?

116. The Seine _____

117. The Don _____

118. The Po River _____

119. The Thames _____

120. The Tiber River _____

121. The River Jordan _____

122. The Murray River _____

123. The River Avon _____

124. The Rhine _____

125. The Mersey River _____

TEST 7J
WHERE DO THEY LIVE?

WHERE IN THE
WORLD MIGHT THE
FOLLOWING PEOPLES
BE FOUND? IDENTIFY
BY STATE OR
COUNTRY.

126. Maoris _____

127. Ainu _____

128. Lapps _____

129. Cajuns _____

130. Basques _____

131. Seminoles _____

132. Zulus _____

133. Aleuts _____

134. Jivaro _____

135. Berbers _____

Geography is much more than listings of names and places. Geography determines culture, prefigures war and conflict, and demonstrates the undeniable linkages of all life on this planet.

But knowing where things are is perhaps the best first step toward greater understanding of all the other things geography represents. It is worth your time to look through a good world atlas. It is amazing just how much these maps and names yield—to the imagination, and to the understanding of that bewildering barrage of names and places we are met with each day.

TEST 7A ANSWERS

1. München is better known to Americans as Munich and is located in Germany.

2. Wien is better known to Americans as Vienna and is located in Austria.

3. Formosa is also known as Taiwan and is located in the Taiwan Strait.

4. Luzern is better known to Americans as Lucerne and is located in Switzerland.

5. Baile Átha Cliath is better known as Dublin and is located in Ireland.

6. Praha is better known in the West as Prague and is located in Czechoslovakia.

7. Moskva is better known in the English-speaking world as Moscow and is located in the Soviet Union.

8. Lisboa is known to Americans as Lisbon and is located in Portugal.

9. Kampuchea is more commonly known in America as Cambodia.

10. Beograd is known to Americans as Belgrade and is located in Yugoslavia.

11. Krung Thep is the name by which Bangkok is known by its inhabitants. It's located in Thailand.

12. Eire is the place we call Ireland.

13. Köln is better known to Americans as Cologne and is located in Germany.

14. Athínai is what the Greek people call this city. It is better known to us as Athens.

15. Persia is the ancient name for Iran.

16. Hades is better known as Hell.

17. Bucureşti is called Bucharest on the evening news. It is located in Romania.

18. Ho Chi Minh City used to be known as Saigon and is located in Vietnam.

19. Napoli is, of course, another way of saying Naples, which is located in Italy. People there are known as Neapolitans.

20. Venezia is what the Italian people call Venice.

TEST 7B ANSWERS

21. Ottumwa is in the state of Iowa

22. Winnemucca is in the state of Nevada

23. Yakima is in the state of Washington

24. Tuscaloosa is in the state of Alabama

25. Peoria is in the state of Illinois

26. Minneapolis is in the state of Minnesota

27. Pensacola is in the state of Florida

28. Pocatello is in the state of Idaho

29. Milwaukee is in the state of Wisconsin

30. Ocala is in the state of Florida

31. Harlem is in New York and was named by settlers from Haarlem in the Netherlands.

32. Ithaca is in New York, but was named after this island off the coast of Greece.

33. New Orleans is, of course, in Louisiana, but was named in honor of the city of Orléans in France.

34. Memphis is in Tennessee and is named for a capital of ancient Egypt.

35. Toledo is in Ohio and shares its name with Toledo, Spain.

TEST 7C ANSWERS

36. Waterloo is in the country of Belgium. It was the site of Napoleon's final defeat on June 18, 1815

37. Lourdes is in France. It was the site of Saint Bernadette's vision of the Virgin Mary.

38. Bethlehem is in Jordan. It was the site of Jesus' birth.

39. Gallipoli is in Turkey. It was the site of a major battle of World War I.

40. Harper's Ferry is in the state of West Virginia. It was the site of John Brown's raid on October 16, 1859.

41. Soweto is in South Africa. It is (and was) the site of severe racial violence.

42. Hastings is in the country of England. It was the site of the Norman Conquest in 1066.

43. Sutter's Fort is in the state of California. It was the site of the discovery of gold in 1848.

44. Gettysburg is in the state of Pennsylvania. It was the site of a major Civil War battle (July 1–3, 1863), which ended with "Pickett's Charge," and of Lincoln's famous Gettysburg Address on November 19, 1863.

45. Greenwich is in the country of England. It is the site of the prime meridian (zero longitude).

46. The Bay of Pigs is in Cuba. It was the site of a U.S.-backed attempted invasion of Cuba by anti-Castro rebels in 1961.

47. Loch Ness is in Scotland. It is the site of many reported sightings of the Loch Ness Monster.

48. Donner Pass is in California. It was the site of the ill-fated Donner Party's winter camp in 1846–1847.

49. Selma is in the state of Alabama. It was the site of severe racial conflict in 1965 when Dr. Martin Luther King, Jr., led a voter registration drive there.

50. Tombstone is in the state of Arizona. It was the site of the gunfight at the O.K. Corral in 1881.

51. Auschwitz is in Poland. It was the site of a Nazi extermination camp in World War II.

52. Ticonderoga is in the state of New York. It is the site of Fort Ticonderoga, established in 1755 and restored in 1909.

53. Guernica is in Spain. It was destroyed in 1937 during the Spanish Civil War.

54. Chernobyl is in the Soviet Union. It was the site of an accident at a nuclear power plant in 1986.

55. Fort Sumter is in the state of South Carolina. It was the site of the first shots fired in the Civil War on April 12, 1861.

56. San Juan Hill is in Cuba. It was the site of a battle of the Spanish-American War in 1898 that caused Spain to cede Cuba to the United States.

57. Alcatraz is in the state of California. It was the site of a maximum-security federal prison, known as "The Rock," from 1933 to 1963.

58. Woodstock is in the state of New York. It was the site of a huge music festival in August 1969.

59. Corregidor is in the Philippines. It was the site of a World War II battle in which the Japanese forced the surrender of 10,000 U.S. and Filipino troops.

60. Stonehenge is in England. It is the site of a prehistoric stone monument that may have served as an astrological instrument.

61. Potsdam is in East Germany. It was the site of the Potsdam Conference/Agreement that ultimately led to the division of Germany into two countries.

62. The Somme is a river in France. It was the site of a massive Allied offensive against Germany in 1916 during World War I.

63. Nagasaki is in Japan. It was the site of detonation of the second atomic bomb in Japan at the end of World War II. The bombing occurred on August 9, 1945.

64. Runnymede is in England. It was the site of King John's acceptance of the Magna Carta in 1215.

65. Pompeii is in Italy. It was the site of the eruption of Mount Vesuvius in A.D. 79. Pompeii was buried under the debris of the volcano.

TEST 7D ANSWERS

66. Hannibal is in the state of Missouri and was the birthplace of Mark Twain.

67. Amherst is in the state of Massachusetts and is known as the home of "the belle of Amherst," Emily Dickinson.

68. Liverpool is in England and was where the Beatles came from.

69. Elsinore is in Denmark and is associated with the character of Hamlet.

70. Orléans is in France and is forever associated with Joan of Arc.

TEST 7E ANSWERS

71. Madagascar is an island.

72. Mindanao is an island.

73. Orinoco is a river.

74. Lassen is a mountain.

75. Titicaca is a lake.

76. Sardinia is an island.

77. Mauna Loa is a mountain.

78. Euphrates is a river.

79. Java is an island.

80. Ararat is a mountain.

TEST 7F ANSWERS

81. The West Bank is in Israel.

82. Londonderry is in Northern Ireland, and also in Australia and Canada.

83. Zimbabwe is in Africa.

84. Addis Abbaba is in Ethiopia.

85. Zurich is in Switzerland.

86. Helsinki is in Finland.

87. Nicosia is in Cyprus.

88. Beijing is in China.

89. Bethesda is in Maryland.

90. Teheran is in Iran.

91. Phnom Penh is in Kampuchea, or Cambodia.

92. East Berlin is in The German Democratic Republic.

93. Lesotho is in Africa.

94. Tel Aviv is in Israel.

95. The United Nations is in New York City.

TEST 7G ANSWERS

96. Siam is now Thailand.

97. Constantinople is now Istanbul.

98. Cathay is now China.

99. Persia is now Iran.

100. Abyssinia is now Ethiopia.

101. Mesopotamia is now part of Iraq.

102. Rhodesia is now Zambia and Zimbabwe.

103. Seward's Folly is now Alaska.

104. The Sandwich Islands are now the Hawaiian Islands.

105. The Gadsden Purchase is now part of New Mexico and Arizona.

TEST 7H ANSWERS

106. Savile Row is in London.

107. The Via Veneto is in Rome.

108. Bourbon Street is in New Orleans.

109. Rodeo Drive is in Beverly Hills.

110. The Autobahn is in Germany.

111. Tiananmen Square is in Beijing.

112. The Ginza is in Tokyo.

113. Pennsylvania Avenue is in Washington, D.C.

114. The Loop is in Chicago.

115. Wall Street is in New York City.

TEST 7I ANSWERS

116. The Seine is in France.

117. The Don rivers flow through England, Scotland, France, and the Soviet Union.

118. The Po River is in Italy.

119. The Thames is in England.

120. The Tiber River irrigates Italy.

121. The River Jordan flows through the Near East.

122. The Murray River is in Australia.

123. The River Avon is in England.

124. The Rhine is in Western Europe.

125. The Mersey River is in England.

TEST 7J ANSWERS

126. Maoris live in New Zealand.

127. Ainu live in Japan.

128. Lapps live in Lapland.

129. Cajuns live in Louisiana.

130. Basques live in West Pyrenees.

131. Seminoles live in Florida and Oklahoma.

132. Zulus live in Natal, South Africa.

133. Aleuts live in the Aleutian Islands and parts of Alaska.

134. Jivaro live in Ecuador and Peru.

135. Berbers live in North Africa.

SCORING

Chernobyl, according to one student, is Cher's full name. Beginning from that wildly incorrect answer, scoring this test should prove far less intimidating. Also, considering the curve of geographic ignorance you're testing against, nearly any score on this test will put you well ahead of a great many of your fellow citizens.

There are 135 questions on this test. Score yourself according to a percentage of correct answers.

121–135: Excellent. You know where you are . . . and where a great many other people are, too.

108–120: You've been around the block, and then some. This is still an excellent score by any current measure.

94–107: Still very good indeed. You are not a stranger in a strange land.

67–106: Not bad. You're likely to feel lost less than half the time.

40–66: You know a good deal about where things are, but you might be letting yourself become a bit too provincial.

39 or fewer: Consult an atlas immediately. Much of what has gone on and is going on will remain mysterious until you get a better sense of where things are. Fortunately, geography is easily learned. Too bad you weren't taught it.

CHAPTER EIGHT

IMMORTAL WORDS AND FAMILIAR PHRASES

Bon mots, the French call them—felicitous phrases and apt ideas that cling to our memories whether we want them to or not. Some give expression to common experience, provide corollaries to our daily experience. Some help us explain things to ourselves. Others simply replay themselves in our minds and in our conversations. They become the things we say when we cannot think of what to say. Endlessly repeated, they provide linkages in our conversation; they anchor ideas and experience in clarifying and unifying context.

The context is clarified when we understand the source of these commonly used expressions and phrases. It is one thing to nod knowingly as a way of masking not knowing; it is another to be full party to what you hear and read.

Knowing the source or association connected to each of the phrases on this next test will not ensure that all that you read or hear will become clear, nor will the absence of knowing disqualify you from reasoned and reasonable conversation—but isn't knowing always preferable to not knowing?

Many of the "immortal words" on this test are drawn from pop culture—from advertising, music, movies. Other questions are drawn from a rich literary and cultural tradition that stretches back to the Greeks, or even further. Some test takers who are vague about the pop culture questions will perhaps argue that a point scale giving the same weight to a quote from Shakespeare as it gives to a jingle from a TV commercial is hopelessly out of balance, weak on the judgment of the relative value of knowing. Some ideas, of course, are more significant or profound than others, and some of the listed quotes embody no ideas at all. But we know what we know, and what we know we tend to use.

You've heard these ideas and phrases before. Do you know where they came from or the associations they make?

TEST 8A
IMMORTAL WORDS AND FAMILIAR PHRASES

WHO SAID (OR IS MOST OFTEN ASSOCIATED WITH) THE FOLLOWING?

1. "I am not a crook." _____

2. "I never met a man I didn't like." _____

3. "A rose is a rose is a rose." _____

4. "A rose by any other name would smell as sweet." _____

_____

5. "Go ahead, make my day." _____

6. "Stifle yourself, Edith." _____

7. "I think, therefore I am." _____

8. "Old soldiers never die; they just fade away." _____

_____

9. "Ich bin ein Berliner." _____

10. "A chicken in every pot . . ." _____

11. "You ain't heard nothin' yet." _____

12. "Mr. Watson, come here, I want you." _____

13. "All the world's a stage . . ." _____

14. "Don't give up the ship." _____

15. "These are the times that try men's souls." _____

16. "Power corrupts, and absolute power corrupts absolutely."

_____

17. "An apple a day keeps the doctor away." _____

18. "Yaba-daba-doo." _____

19. "Give me liberty, or give me death." _____

20. "Reports of my death have been greatly exaggerated." _____

_____

21. "This is another fine mess you've gotten me into." _____

_____

22. "It's a bird, it's a plane, it's _____"

23. "I cannot tell a lie."_____

24. "C'mon up sometime, and see me." _____

25. "Return with us now to those thrilling days of yesteryear."

_____

26. "The fog creeps in on little cat feet." _____

27. "What does woman want?" _____

28. "Love means never having to say you're sorry." _____

_____

29. "Let them eat cake." _____ _____

30. "There are no second acts in American life." _____

31. "A penny saved is a penny earned." _____

32. " 'Scuse me while I kiss the sky (this guy)." _____

33. "Tyger, tyger, burning bright." _____

34. "Take my wife . . . please." _____

35. "Never have so many owed so much to so few." _____

_____

36. "Truth is beauty; beauty truth. That's all ye know, and all

ye need to know." _____

37. "Anyone who hates children and dogs can't be all bad."

_____

38. "By the shore of Gitche Gumee . . ." _____

39. "The best laid plans of mice and men oft go awry" (or "aft

gang agley") _____

40. "United we stand, divided we fall." _____

41. "What's up, Doc?" _____

42. "Good night, sweet Prince." _____

43. "To boldly go where no man has gone before." _____

44. "You ain't nothin' but a hound dog." _____

45. "This doesn't look like Kansas." _____

46. "December 7—a day which will live in infamy." _____

47. "Frankly, my dear, I don't give a damn." _____

48. "Theirs not to reason why, theirs but to do or die." _____

_____

49. "Won't you be my neighbor." _____

50. "How do you spell relief?" _____

51. "I have always depended upon the kindness of strangers."

_____

52. "Quitting smoking is easy. I've done it hundreds of times."

_____

53. "War is hell." _____

54. "It is lucky that war is so terrible, else we should grow to

love it too much." _____

55. "I think that I shall never see a poem lovely as a tree."

_____

56. "Rosebud." _____

57. "I could have been a contender." _____

58. "Play it again, Sam." _____

59. "We made him an offer he couldn't refuse." _____

60. "All is for the best in the best of all possible worlds." _____

_____

61. "From each according to his ability; to each according to

his need." _____

62. "And that's the way it is." _____

63. "Float like a butterfly, sting like a bee." _____

64. "Dr. Livingstone, I presume." _____

65. "I have a dream." _____

66. "God bless us, everyone." _____

67. "I saw the best minds of my generation destroyed by

madness, starving, hysterical, naked." _____

68. "It's not easy being green." _____

69. "'Twas brillig, and the slithy toves did gyre and gimble in

the wabe . . ." _____

70. "I'm not afraid of death; I just don't want to be there when

it happens." _____

71. "Just say no." _____

72. "I know you are, but what am I?" _____

73. "Isn't that special." _____

74. "And so it goes." _____

75. "Are you now, or have you ever been, a member of the

Communist party?" _____

76. "Do unto others as you would have them do unto you."

_____

77. "Call me Ishmael." _____

78. "Neither a borrower nor a lender be." _____

79. "Fourscore and seven years ago." _____

80. "Our Father, who art in heaven." _____

81. "When in the course of human events . . ." _____

82. "Catch-22." _____

83. "Girls just wanna have fun." _____

84. "I'm a material girl." _____

85. "Who knows what evil lurks in the hearts of men." _____

_____

86. "Say good night, Gracie." _____

87. "That's one small step for a man, one giant leap for

mankind." _____

88. "Twas the night before Christmas, and all through the

house . . ." _____

89. "You supply the stories; I'll supply the war." _____

_____

90. "Go west, young man." _____

91. "How sweet it is." _____

92. "How do I love thee? Let me count the ways." _____

93. "Elementary, my dear Watson." _____

94. ". . . And miles to go before I sleep." _____

95. "Heeere's Johnny." _____

96. "You can fool all of the people some of the time, some of the people all of the time, but you can't fool all of the people all of the time." _____

97. "Take the A Train." _____

98. "The business of America is business." _____

99. ". . . in spite of everything I still believe that people are really good at heart." _____

100. "This land is your land. This land is my land. . . . This land was made for you and me." _____

101. "If you've seen one redwood tree, you've seen them all." _____

102. "From where the sun now stands I will fight no more, forever." _____

103. "All for one, and one for all." _____

104. "The police aren't there to create disorder; the police are there to preserve disorder." _____

105. "My name is Captain Spaulding." _____

106. "Round up the usual suspects." _____

107. "Veni, vidi, vici." _____

108. "Extremism in the pursuit of liberty is no vice." _____

109. "Good night, Irene, good night . . ." _____

110. "Things are more the way they are now than they've ever been before." _____

111. "The answer, my friend, is blowin' in the wind." _____

112. "Workers of the world, unite." _____

113. "Born in the U.S.A." _____

114. "Quoth the Raven, nevermore." _____

115. "On the road again." _____

116. "Way down upon the Swanee River." _____

117. "No one ever went broke underestimating the intelligence of the American people." _____

118. "Television is a vast wasteland." _____

119. "Abandon all hope, ye who enter here." _____

120. "That's all, folks." _____

But, of course, that's not all. Many more questions of this sort soon await you. But before we move on to those new challenges, it's worth noting that some of the sources of those famous phrases you've just gone through were fairly obscure. Although you'd surely heard most of the phrases, you might not have known who said them, or in what context. Frankly, some of the more obscure questions were included because the sources reveal some interesting episodes and attitudes worth remembering.

The next set of questions should prove somewhat easier. In this series, the sources are provided. All you have to do is supply the part of the phrase that has been left out. Since these phrases are so ubiquitous, this should prove fairly easy.

TEST 8B
COMPLETE THE THOUGHT

121. According to General Phil Sheridan, "The only good Indian is a _____."

122. Alexander Pope, English poet, wrote that "Hope springs eternal in _____."

123. Noted wit and writer Dorothy Parker lamented that "Men seldom make passes at _____."

124. Edgar Guest observed that "It takes a heap of livin' to make a _____."

125. "History is _____," according to Henry Ford.

126. Nelson Algren sagely advised: "Never eat at a place called _____; never play poker with a man named _____. Never go to bed with a woman whose troubles are _____

_____."

127. English poet William Wordsworth wrote that "The child is father to _____."

128. Ralph Waldo Emerson said that "A foolish consistency is the hobgoblin of _____."

129. "Oh, what a tangled web we weave when _____

_____," wrote English novelist Sir Walter Scott.

130. In Lincoln's second inaugural address, he promised

"Malice toward none; with _____."

131. Humorist Josh Billings supplied us with the oft-repeated

observation that "The wheel that squeaks the loudest is the

_____."

132. Roman gladiators were quite magnanimous in saying, "We

who are about to die _____."

133. English poet Rudyard Kipling asserted that "The female

of the species is _____ than the male."

134. Something of a misogynist, Kipling also wrote that "A

woman is only a woman, but a good cigar is a _____."

135. On a good day, Robert Louis Stevenson wrote, "The world

is so full of a number of things, I'm sure we should all be

_____."

136. In his "Ode to the West Wind," Shelley wrote, "If winter

comes can _____."

137. Pliny, who knew much, observed "In vino veritas," which

means that "In wine, there is _____."

138. Hamlet, disgruntled, opined, "Frailty, thy name is _____."

139. The Duke of Wellington said that "The battle of Waterloo was won on the _____."

140. Milton gave heart to rationalizers everywhere when he wrote, "They also serve who only _____."

141. George Bernard Shaw observed that "He who can, does; he who cannot, _____."

142. Disraeli, British Prime Minister, grouped lies into three categories: "Lies, damned lies, and _____."

143. "Religion," according to Karl Marx, "is the _____ _____."

144. "Patriotism," according to Samuel Johnson, "is the last _____."

145. Theodore Roosevelt urged the United States to "Speak softly, and carry a _____."

146. "Water, water everywhere," wrote poet Samuel Taylor Coleridge, then added, "_____."

147. In the words of the Jewish proverb, "God could not be everywhere and therefore he made _____."

148. Robert Browning, also on a good day, wrote, "God's in his Heaven/All's right _____."

149. Samuel Smiles, in praise of order, wrote, "There's a place for everything and _____."

150. Philosopher Santayana intoned those oft-repeated words, "Those who cannot remember the past are _____ _____."

151. "Parting," lamented Juliet, "is such _____."

152. Lord Byron praised a lady, writing, "She walks in beauty like _____."

153. Accepting the Nobel Prize in 1949, William Faulkner said that he believed "Man will not merely endure. He will _____."

154. Somewhat disingenuously, Will Rogers said, "All I know is what I _____."

155. Even before zip codes, Herodotus wrote that "Neither snow, nor rain, nor heat, nor gloom of night can _____ _____."

156. Samuel Goldwyn, famous for malapropisms, said that "Verbal contracts aren't worth the _____."

157. Henry Wadsworth Longfellow observed that "Into each life some _____."

158. Longfellow also wrote of having "shot an arrow into the air" which "_____."

159. A popular expression in the 1960s advised: "Don't trust anyone _____."

160. Benjamin Franklin, who contributed dozens of aphorisms to our daily discourse, wrote that "In this world nothing is certain but death and _____."

161. Franklin also advocated the following regimen, long before our current fitness craze. "Early to bed and early to rise, makes a man _____, _____, and _____."

162. Also, thanks to Franklin, we know and often repeat that "An ounce of prevention is worth a _____."

163. Football coach Vince Lombardi may or may not have actually said that "Winning isn't everything. It's the _____ _____."

164. Lighthorse Harry Lee said of George Washington, "First in war, first in peace, and first in _____ _____."

165. Early in his songwriting career, Bob Dylan cautioned, "Don't follow leaders, watch the _____."

166. Franklin Roosevelt, a generation earlier, had assured us that "The only thing we have to fear is _____."

167. According to philosopher Hobbes, "Knowledge is _____."

168. In *Twelfth Night*, Shakespeare wrote, "If music be the

food of love, _____."

169. The pirates in Robert Louis Stevenson's *Treasure Island*

sang of "Fifteen men on the dead man's chest, Yo ho ho and a

_____."

170. Greta Garbo is famous for her line "I want to be _____."

TEST 8C
BIBLICAL PHRASES

171. "For the love of money is the _____

_____." (Timothy, 6:10)

172. "It is easier for a camel to pass through the eye of a

needle than for a _____."
(Matthew, 19:24)

173. "He that is without sin among you, let him _____

_____." (John, 8:7)

174. "The wages of sin is _____." (Romans 6:23)

175. ". . . they that shall take the sword shall perish by _____

_____." (Matthew 26:52)

176. "Lead us not into temptation, but _____

_____." (Matthew 6:13)

177. "A virtuous woman is a crown to _____."
(Proverbs 12:4)

DON'T GET NERVOUS. IF YOU'RE NOT PARTICULARLY RELIGIOUS, YOU CAN STILL DO WELL ON THE UPCOMING SECTION OF THIS TEST. CHRISTIAN, JEW, MUSLIM, OR ATHEIST, WE ALL LIVE IN A CULTURE INFUSED WITH THE WORDS AND WISDOM OF THE BIBLE. IT IS UNLIKELY THAT THE PHRASES IN THIS PART OF THE TEST WILL BE NEW TO YOU. EVEN IF YOU'VE NEVER OPENED THE BOOK, I'LL WAGER YOU'LL DO WELL ON THIS TEST. COMPLETE THE FOLLOWING PHRASES.

178. "For they have sown the wind, and they shall reap _____

_____." (Hosea 8:7)

179. "A soft answer turneth away _____." (Proverbs 15:1)

180. "If God is for us, who _____."
(Romans 8:31)

TEST 8D
IT PAYS TO ADVERTISE

TRY TO REMEMBER YOUR SOCIAL SECURITY NUMBER OR AN IMPORTANT ANNIVERSARY AND LIKE AS NOT YOU'LL COME UP EMPTY, BUT JUST TRY TO GET RID OF AN ADVERTISING JINGLE ONCE IT'S IN YOUR HEAD. ADVERTISERS SPEND VAST SUMS OF MONEY TRYING TO MAKE THEIR MESSAGES STICK, AND QUITE OFTEN THEY'RE MORE SUCCESSFUL AT IT THAN WE'D LIKE THEM TO BE. (WHO WOULD EVER HAVE IMAGINED THAT THIS STUFF WOULD COME IN HANDY ONE DAY?)

WHAT PRODUCTS WERE THE FOLLOWING LINES USED TO SELL?

181. "I'd like to buy the world a _____."

182. "Does she or doesn't she? Only her hairdresser knows for

sure." _____

183. "I can't believe I ate the whole thing." _____

184. "From the land of sky blue waters." _____

185. "Promise her anything, but give her _____."

186. "You'll wonder where the yellow went when you brush

your teeth with _____."

187. "Progress is our most important product." _____

188. "A little dab'll do ya." _____

189. "I liked it so much I bought the company." _____

190. "When you care enough to send the very best." _____

191. "I'd walk a mile for a _____."

192. "99 and 44/100% pure." _____

193. "LSMFT" _____

194. "I dreamed I was a Princess . . . in my _____

_____."

195. "See the USA in your _____."

196. "Nothin' says lovin' like somethin' from the oven, and

_____ says it best."

197. "Inquiring minds want to know." _____

198. "Better living through chemistry." _____

199. "_____, the San Francisco treat."

200. "_____, hits the spot, eight full ounces, that's a lot."

TEST 8E
FOREIGN, YET FAMILIAR

201. Tempus fugit _____

202. Tabula rasa _____

203. Quid pro quo _____

204. In utero _____

205. Pro forma _____

206. Sine qua non _____

207. Prima facie _____

208. Caveat Emptor _____

209. Joie de vivre _____

210. C'est la guerre _____

211. Noblesse oblige _____

212. Avant-garde _____

213. Enfant terrible _____

214. Potpourri _____

OUR DISCOURSE, SPOKEN AND WRITTEN, IS ALSO LARDED WITH PHRASES FROM OTHER LANGUAGES, TERMS WE BORROW WITHOUT TRANSLATION BECAUSE THE MEANINGS ARE CLEAR AND UNIVERSAL. IT IS UNLIKELY THAT YOU COULD READ A NEWSPAPER, LISTEN TO THE RADIO, OR WATCH TELEVISION FOR VERY LONG WITHOUT ENCOUNTERING ONE OR MORE OF THE FOLLOWING COMMONLY USED BORROWINGS FROM OTHER TONGUES. DO YOU KNOW WHAT THEY MEAN?

215. Zeitgeist _____

216. Sturm and Drang _____

217. Weltschmerz _____

218. Lumpen proletariat _____

219. Que será será _____

220. Chutzpah _____

So, for the purpose of testing your knowledge and memory of the phrases that fuel daily discourse, "our revels are ended." Check your answers and discover what you knew and didn't know about these common phrases.

TEST 8A ANSWERS

1. "I am not a crook." Richard Nixon

2. "I never met a man I didn't like." Will Rogers

3. "A rose is a rose is a rose." Gertrude Stein

4. "A rose by any other name would smell as sweet." William Shakespeare

5. "Go ahead, make my day." Clint Eastwood as Dirty Harry

6. "Stifle yourself, Edith." Carroll O'Connor as Archie Bunker

7. "I think, therefore I am." Philosopher René Descartes

8. "Old soldiers never die; they just fade away." General MacArthur

9. "Ich bin ein Berliner." President John F. Kennedy

10. "A chicken in every pot . . ." Herbert Hoover

11. "You ain't heard nothin' yet." Al Jolson in the first talkie

12. "Mr. Watson, come here . . ." Alexander Graham Bell

13. "All the world's a stage . . ." William Shakespeare

14. "Don't give up the ship." John Paul Jones

15. "These are the times that try men's souls." Citizen Tom Paine

16. "Power corrupts, and absolute power . . ." Lord Acton

17. "An apple a day . . ." Benjamin Franklin

18. "Yaba-daba-doo." Fred Flintstone

19. "Give me liberty, or give me death." Patrick Henry

20. "Reports of my death have been greatly exaggerated." Mark Twain

21. "This is another fine mess you've gotten me into." Oliver Hardy

22. "It's a bird, it's a plane, it's Superman."

23. "I cannot tell a lie." George Washington

24. "C'mon up sometime, and see me." Mae West

25. "Return with us now to those thrilling days of yesteryear." *The Lone Ranger* radio show

26. "The fog creeps in on little cat feet." Carl Sandburg

27. "What does woman want?" Sigmund Freud

28. "Love means never having to say you're sorry." *Love Story* by Erich Segal

29. "Let them eat cake." Marie Antoinette

30. "There are no second acts in American life." F. Scott Fitzgerald

31. "A penny saved is a penny earned." Benjamin Franklin

32. " ''cuse me while I kiss the sky (this guy)." Jimi Hendrix

33. "Tyger, tyger, burning bright." William Blake

34. "Take my wife . . . please." Henny Youngman

35. "Never have so many owed so much . . ." Winston Churchill

36. "Truth is beauty; beauty truth. That's all ye know, and all ye need to know." John Keats

37. "Anyone who hates children and dogs can't be all bad." Attributed to W. C. Fields

38. "By the shore of Gitche Gumee . . ." Longfellow

39. "The best laid plans of mice and men oft go awry." Robert Burns

40. "United we stand, divided we fall." Abraham Lincoln

41. "What's up, Doc?" Bugs Bunny

42. "Good night, sweet Prince." Shakespeare, *Hamlet*

43. "To boldly go where no man has gone before." *Star Trek*

44. "You ain't nothin' but a hound dog." Big Mama Thornton/ Elvis Presley

45. "This doesn't look like Kansas." Dorothy in *The Wizard of Oz*

46. "December 7—a day which will live in infamy." Franklin D. Roosevelt

47. "Frankly, my dear, I don't give a damn." Rhett Butler in *Gone With the Wind*

48. "Theirs not to reason why, theirs but to do or die." Alfred Lord Tennyson, "The Charge of the Light Brigade"

49. "Won't you be my neighbor." Mr. Rogers

50. "How do you spell relief?" Rolaids ad

51. "I have always depended upon the kindness of strangers." Blanche Dubois in *A Streetcar Named Desire*

52. "Quitting smoking is easy. I've done it hundreds of times." Mark Twain

53. "War is hell." William Tecumseh Sherman

54. "It is lucky that war is so terrible, else we should grow to love it too much." Robert E. Lee

55. "I think that I shall never see a poem lovely as a tree." Joyce Kilmer

56. "Rosebud." Famous line from *Citizen Kane*

57. "I could have been a contender." Marlon Brando as Terry Malloy in *On the Waterfront*

58. "Play it again, Sam." Thought to have been Humphrey Bogart's line in *Casablanca*. It wasn't.

59. "We made him an offer he couldn't refuse." From *The Godfather*

60. "All is for the best in the best of all possible worlds." Voltaire, *Candide*

61. "From each according to his ability; to each according to his need." Karl Marx

62. "And that's the way it is." Walter Cronkite

63. "Float like a butterfly, sting like a bee." Muhammad Ali

64. "Dr. Livingstone, I presume." Henry Stanley

65. "I have a dream." Martin Luther King, Jr.

66. "God bless us, everyone." Tiny Tim, from Dickens' *A Christmas Carol*

67. "I saw the best minds of my generation destroyed by madness, starving, hysterical, naked." Allen Ginsberg, from "Howl"

68. "It's not easy being green." Kermit the frog

69. "'Twas brillig, and the slithy toves did gyre and gimble in the wabe . . ." "Jabberwocky," Lewis Carroll

70. "I'm not afraid of death; I just don't want to be there when it happens." Woody Allen

71. "Just say no." Antidrug slogan associated with Nancy Reagan

72. "I know you are, but what am I?" Pee Wee Herman

73. "Isn't that special." Dana Carvey, The Church Lady

74. "And so it goes." Linda Ellerbee, from Kurt Vonnegut's *Slaughterhouse Five*

75. "Are you now, or have you ever been, a member of the Communist party?" Senator Joseph McCarthy

76. "Do unto others as you would have them do unto you." The Golden Rule

77. "Call me Ishmael." Herman Melville, the opening line of *Moby-Dick*

78. "Neither a borrower nor a lender be." Shakespeare, *Hamlet*

79. "Fourscore and seven years ago." Lincoln, Gettysburg Address

80. "Our Father, who art in heaven." The Lord's Prayer

81. "When in the course of human events . . ." Declaration of Independence

82. "Catch-22" Joseph Heller

83. "Girls just wanna have fun." Cyndi Lauper

84. "I'm a material girl." Madonna

85. "Who knows what evil lurks in the hearts of men." The Shadow radio show

86. "Say good night, Gracie." George Burns/Gracie Allen

87. "That's one small step for a man, one giant leap for mankind." Neil Armstrong on the moon

88. " 'Twas the night before Christmas, and all through the house . . ." C. Clement Moore

89. "You supply the stories, I'll supply the war." William Randolph Hearst to war correspondents before the Spanish-American War

90. "Go west, young man." Newspaperman Horace Greeley

91. "How sweet it is." Jackie Gleason

92. "How do I love thee?" Elizabeth Barrett Browning, Sonnet 43

93. "Elementary, my dear Watson." Sherlock Holmes, created by Sir Arthur Conan Doyle

94. ". . . And miles to go before I sleep." Robert Frost

95. "Heeere's Johnny." Ed McMahon of *The Tonight Show*.

96. "You can fool all of the people some of the time, some of the people all of the time, but you can't fool all of the people all of the time." Abraham Lincoln

97. "Take the A Train." Duke Ellington

98. "The business of America is business." Calvin Coolidge

99. ". . . in spite of everything I still believe that people are really good at heart." Anne Frank

100. "This land is your land. This land is my land. . . . This land was made for you and me." Woody Guthrie

101. "If you've seen one redwood tree, you've seen them all." Ronald Reagan

102. "From where the sun now stands I will fight no more, forever." Chief Joseph of the Nez Percé.

103. "All for one, and one for all." The Three Musketeers, created by Alexandre Dumas

104. "The police aren't there to create disorder; the police are

there to preserve disorder." Mayor Richard Daley, Chicago, 1968

105. "My name is Captain Spaulding." Groucho Marx

106. "Round up the usual suspects." Claude Rains as Capt. Renault in *Casablanca*

107. "Veni, vidi, vici." Julius Caesar

108. "Extremism in the pursuit of liberty . . ." Barry Goldwater

109. "Good night, Irene, good night . . ." Huddie Ledbetter (Leadbelly)

110. "Things are more the way they are now than they've ever been before." President Dwight Eisenhower

111. "The answer, my friend, is blowin' in the wind." Bob Dylan

112. "Workers of the world, unite." Marx and Engels

113. "Born in the U.S.A." Bruce Springsteen

114. "Quoth the Raven, 'Nevermore.'" Edgar Allan Poe

115. "On the road again." Willie Nelson

116. "Way down upon the Swanee River." Stephen Foster

117. "No one ever went broke underestimating the intelligence of American people." P. T. Barnum

118. "Television is a vast wasteland." Newton Minnow, F.C.C.

119. "Abandon all hope, ye who enter here." From Dante's *The Inferno*

120. "That's all, folks." Porky Pig, Warner Bros.

TEST 8B ANSWERS

121. "The only good Indian is a dead Indian."

122. "Hope springs eternal in the human breast."

123. "Men seldom make passes at girls who wear glasses."

124. "It takes a heap of livin' to make a house a home."

125. "History is bunk."

126. "Never eat at a place called Mom's; never play poker with a man named Doc. Never go to bed with a woman whose troubles are worse than your own."

127. "The child is father to the man."

128. "A foolish consistency is the hobgoblin of little minds."

129. "Oh, what a tangled web we weave when first we practice to deceive."

130. "Malice toward none; with charity toward all."

131. "The wheel that squeaks the loudest is the one that gets the grease."

132. "We who are about to die salute you."

133. "The female of the species is deadlier than the male."

134. "A woman is only a woman, but a good cigar is a smoke."

135. "The world is so full of a number of things, I'm sure we should all be as happy as kings."

136. "If winter comes can spring be far behind?"

137. "In wine, there is truth."

138. "Frailty, thy name is woman."

139. "The battle of Waterloo was won on the playing fields of Eton."

140. "They also serve who only stand and wait."

141. "He who can, does; he who cannot, teaches."

142. "Lies, damned lies, and statistics."

143. "Religion is the opiate of the masses."

144. "Patriotism is the last refuge of the scoundrel."

145. "Speak softly, and carry a big stick."

146. "Water, water everywhere, nor any drop to drink."

147. "God could not be everywhere and therefore he made mothers."

148. "God's in his Heaven/All's right with the world."

149. "There's a place for everything, and everything in its place."

150. "Those who cannot remember the past are doomed to repeat it."

151. "Parting is such sweet sorrow."

152. "She walks in beauty like the night."

153. "Man will not merely endure. He will prevail."

154. "All I know is what I read in the newspapers."

155. "Neither snow, nor rain, nor heat, nor gloom of night can stay these couriers from the swift completion of their appointed rounds."

156. "Verbal contracts aren't worth the paper they're written on."

157. "Into each life some rain must fall."

158. "I shot an arrow into the air; it fell to earth, I knew not where."

159. "Don't trust anyone over thirty."

160. "In this world nothing is certain but death and taxes."

161. "Early to bed and early to rise, makes a man healthy, wealthy, and wise."

162. "An ounce of prevention is worth a pound of cure."

163. "Winning isn't everything. It's the only thing."

164. "First in war, first in peace, and first in the hearts of his countrymen."

165. "Don't follow leaders, watch the parking meters."

166. "The only thing we have to fear is fear itself."

167. "Knowledge is power."

168. "If music be the food of love, play on."

169. "Fifteen men on the dead man's chest, Yo ho ho and a bottle of rum."

170. "I want to be alone."

TEST 8C ANSWERS

171. "For the love of money is the root of all evil."

172. "It is easier for a camel to pass through the eye of a needle than for a rich man to enter the kingdom of heaven."

173. "He that is without sin among you, let him cast the first stone."

174. "The wages of sin is death."

175. ". . . they that shall take the sword shall perish by the sword."

176. "Lead us not into temptation, but deliver us from evil."

177. "A virtuous woman is a crown to her husband."

178. "For they have sown the wind, and they shall reap the whirlwind."

179. "A soft answer turneth away wrath."

180. "If God is for us, who can be against us."

TEST 8D ANSWERS

181. "I'd like to buy the world a Coke."

182. "Does she or doesn't she? Only her hairdresser knows for sure." Clairol

183. "I can't believe I ate the whole thing." Alka-Seltzer

184. "From the land of sky blue waters." Pabst Blue Ribbon Beer

185. "Promise her anything, but give her Arpege."

186. "You'll wonder where the yellow went when you brush your teeth with Pepsodent."

187. "Progress is our most important product." General Electric

188. "A little dab'll do ya." Brylcreem hair cream

189. "I liked it so much I bought the company." Remington shavers

190. "When you care enough to send the very best." Hallmark Cards

191. "I'd walk a mile for a Camel."

192. "99 and $^{44}/_{100}$% pure." Ivory Soap

193. "LSMFT" Lucky Strike Means Fine Tobaccos

194. "I dreamed I was a Princess . . . in my Maidenform bra."

195. "See the USA in your Chevrolet."

196. "Nothin' says lovin' like somethin' from the oven, and Pillsbury says it best."

197. "Inquiring minds want to know." The *National Enquirer*

198. "Better living through chemistry." Dupont

199. "Rice-A-Roni, the San Francisco treat."

200. "Pepsi-Cola hits the spot, eight full ounces, that's a lot."

TEST 8E ANSWERS

201. Tempus fugit is Latin for *time flies.*

202. Tabula rasa is Latin for *blank slate.*

203. Quid pro quo is Latin for *something in return.*

204. In utero is Latin for *in the womb.*

205. Pro forma is Latin for *done in a perfunctory or formal way;* literally, "for the sake of form."

206. Sine qua non is Latin for *a necessity, an indispensable condition;* literally, "without which not."

207. Prima facie is Latin for *at first view; on first impression.*

208. Caveat emptor is Latin for *let the buyer beware.*

209. Joie de vivre is French for *joy of living.*

210. C'est la guerre is French for *that is war.*

211. Noblesse oblige is French for *rank imposes obligations.*

212. Avant-garde is French for *vanguard.*

213. Enfant terrible is French for *terrible child.*

214. Potpourri is French for *a stew or a mixture of things.*

215. Zeitgeist is German for *the spirit of the times.*

216. Sturm and Drang is German for *storm and stress, unrest.*

217. Weltschmerz is German for *world sadness, pessimistic melancholy.*

218. Lumpen proletariat is German for *poor workers.*

219. Que será será is Spanish for *what will be, will be.*

220. Chutzpah is Yiddish for *brazenness or gall.*

SCORING

Because most of these phrases are so ubiquitous, a high score is expected from you here.

198–220: You are a retentive cliché monger, but you also know your sources. Chances are, you're seldom out of your depth in any conversation.

176–197: That's more than good enough. About 20 percent of these questions were either somewhat obscure as to source, fleeting as to significance, or the kinds of things you might easily have avoided hearing. In any event, you know a great deal, and surely you know much more than the test drew upon.

154–175: Still good. And you've got the advantage and the opportunity to learn nearly 30 percent more than you knew before. Some of it may not seem worth knowing, but by the time you decide that, you'll already know it.

110–153: Not too bad, but stick around. Many of these phrases are certain to become familiar as you spend more days on the planet. Some of them you're almost certain to hear again within days of hearing them for the first time.

66–109: You probably need to read more, but you should not despair. Many of these phrases are far from profound.

22–65: Are you from around these parts? If you scored in the 10 to 30 percent range, you've either emigrated here recently or you just haven't been paying attention. In any event, this brief list is just the merest beginning of the catch phrases you'll probably want to catch up on.

CHAPTER NINE

DEEDS AND THE DOERS OF DEEDS

Deeds are generally considered to be more important than words, but it is through words that deeds are remembered. In books and in speech, we pass down the deeds we admire and the deeds we abhor. Much of what is in this book is a matter of testing your knowledge of deeds that people in our culture have generally considered important and worth remembering.

As this book began to take shape, however, certain underlying assumptions became clear. Much of what we have chosen to remember about the activities of our ancestors has a decidedly male slant. If it's common knowledge, it's more likely to be about the achievements of a male than about a female. This male slant not only has afforded men greater opportunities for the sorts of accomplishments we tend to glorify and remember, it has also defined what kinds of achievements and contributions are worthy of recording for history.

The tests in this book reflect certain cultural biases, and for that reason it turns out that there are far more males than females who serve as a basis for the test items. At some point in preparing these tests I came to realize this and to anticipate the criticism that the tests were sexist. The criticism is just. In selecting questions for these tests, I usually employed the criterion of common knowledge. For the aforementioned and other reasons, the contributions made by women have been slighted.

The tests are probably also biased in favor of test takers who have lived longer. Reasonably alert and intelligent people who have lived longer than other reasonably alert and intelligent people will in all likelihood do better on these tests. That, it seems, is as it should be. After all, if we are alive to the world at all, the years should give us something, pay some dividend. Testing is seldom fair, and it is probable that on any single test in this book, someone who is twenty years older should do roughly 20 percent better than a younger counterpart.

Does the world grade on a curve? You bet it does. Many of our failings are forgiven because of compensatory strengths. Does the best test score always indicate the best student or the best mind in the sample? Hardly; that's a testing myth. Such mythology leads to any number of self-fulfilling prophecies that influence how people think about themselves and how they conduct their lives. Testing in its many academic forms normally is a fault-finding exercise that as often as not gets in the way of learning and inhibits rather than encourages an otherwise normal human curiosity.

Confucius, remembered and revered for his wisdom, would not pass any of the tests in this book. In fact, he would fail miserably, would score far lower than the most dismal "underachiever" in the country's worst school. And yet it was Confucius, half a thousand years before the birth of Christ, who asked, "Shall I teach you what knowledge is? When you know a thing, to hold that you know it; and when you don't know a thing, to allow that you don't know it. That is knowledge." The nearly two thousand questions in this book allow you to establish when you know a thing and, perhaps more significantly, when you don't know a thing. Once you establish that, you can begin if you wish to acquire more knowledge to hold.

Do these tests, then, provide any kind of comprehensive measure of all that should be known? Does every question concern vital or essential knowledge? Is a person who scores 100 percent on all of the tests in this book excused from the necessity of further learning? The obvious answer to all of these questions is an emphatic no. Learning, whether we like it or not, is never-ending, a progression out of darkness toward light. Yet another of the many misperceptions that schools inadvertently teach is the sense that your education ends once you graduate. To the mind that remains alive, no matter the battering it takes in school and out, *learning* is another word for being alive.

TEST 9A
DEEDS AND THE DOERS OF DEEDS

WHO DID, OR IS THOUGHT TO HAVE DONE, THE FOLLOWING:

1. The development of the process of pasteurization _____

2. The first heart transplant _____

3. The discovery of gravity _____

4. The Louisiana Purchase _____

5. Author of *Utopia* who defied Henry VIII _____

6. The discovery of the New World _____

7. The Protestant Reformation _____

8. The formation of the Church of England _____

9. World War II's most decorated U.S. war hero _____

10. The first man on the moon _____

11. The first American to orbit the earth _____

12. The intellectual founders of communism _____

13. The head of the Third Reich _____

14. Two major English romantic poets _____

15. The playwright who wrote *Cymbeline* _____

16. Two painters who founded Cubism _____

17. The two best-known nineteenth-century American feminists _____

18. The first first lady of the United States _____

_____

19. The director of *Birth of a Nation* _____

20. The scientist who postulated that the earth moves around the sun _____

21. The leader of the Norman Conquest _____

22. Author of *On the Origin of Species* _____

23. The "face that launched a thousand ships" _____

24. Inventor of the phonograph _____

25. The theory of relativity _____

26. The author of the Monroe Doctrine _____

27. The creator of Mickey Mouse _____

28. The man credited with devising the assembly line method of industrial production _____

29. Inventor of the wireless radio _____

30. Man in charge of the New Deal _____

31. Father of psychoanalysis _____

32. Assassin of Abraham Lincoln _____

33. World's first four-minute-miler _____

34. Ruler of England at the height of its empire ＿＿＿＿＿＿

35. First solo nonstop transatlantic flight aviator ＿＿＿＿＿＿

36. Best-remembered Greek ruler during the Golden Age

＿＿＿＿＿＿＿＿＿＿＿＿＿＿＿＿＿＿＿＿＿＿＿

37. The Queen of the Nile ＿＿＿＿＿＿＿＿＿＿＿

38. Inventor of the printing press ＿＿＿＿＿＿＿＿

39. Author of *Gulliver's Travels* ＿＿＿＿＿＿＿＿

40. English king during the American Revolution ＿＿＿＿＿

41. Ethiopian King during the Italian invasion ＿＿＿＿＿＿

42. Fascist ruler of Spain during World War II ＿＿＿＿＿＿

43. Director of "Do the Right Thing" ＿＿＿＿＿＿＿

44. *Rite of Spring* composer ＿＿＿＿＿＿＿＿＿

45. Russian Communist leader killed while in exile in Mexico

＿＿＿＿＿＿＿＿＿＿＿＿＿＿＿＿＿＿＿＿＿＿＿

46. Spanish explorer who discovered Florida ＿＿＿＿＿＿

47. Leader of American forces at the Battle of New Orleans

during the War of 1812 ＿＿＿＿＿＿＿＿＿＿＿＿＿＿

48. American woman known as the "Moses of her people" for

helping hundreds of slaves escape to the North on the

Underground Railroad ＿＿＿＿＿＿＿＿＿＿＿＿＿＿

49. Composer most associated with the music known as

ragtime ＿＿＿＿＿＿＿＿＿＿＿＿＿＿＿＿＿＿＿

50. *Time* magazine's "Man of the Decade" for the 1980s _____

51. Woman who became known as the "mother of the civil rights movement" when she refused to give up her seat on a bus in the 1950s _____

52. Black leader of the Back to Africa Movement _____

53. British general who defeated Napoleon at Waterloo _____
_____

54. Persian poet who wrote *Robaiyat (The Rubaiyat)* _____
_____

55. Austrian-Czech author of *The Trial* _____

56. English poet who wrote *The Faerie Queene* _____

57. American author of *The Scarlet Letter* _____

58. Austrian composer of *The Magic Flute* _____

59. U.S. composer of "Stars and Stripes Forever" _____

60. French author of *The Second Sex* _____

61. Central figure in the Savings and Loan Scandal; head of Lincoln Savings _____

62. English author of *Leviathan* _____

63. American author of *Portnoy's Complaint* _____

64. Richard Nixon's opponent in the 1968 presidential race
_____

65. Convicted of slapping a Beverly Hills cop _____

66. Philippine ruler ousted by Corazon Aquino _____

67. Military leader of American forces in Vietnam War _____

_____

68. Russian-born Israeli woman who served as prime minister

of Israel, 1969–1974 _____

_____

69. The Virgin Queen _____

70. The "King of Rock 'n' Roll" _____

71. Founding editor of *Ms.* magazine _____

72. English author of *Middlemarch* _____

73. U.S.-born British poet who penned *The Wasteland* _____

74. Pathfinder who established the Cumberland Trail _____

_____

75. Soviet leader who said, "We will bury you" _____

_____

76. American President who called the Soviet Union "the evil

empire" _____

77. Presidential candidate who wanted us to read his lips _____

_____

78. Man who stood in the door of the University of Alabama

registration office to block integration _____

79. Famous British nurse during the Crimean War _____

_____

80. VP candidate who was "no Jack Kennedy" _____

81. Leader of an uprising of gladiators in Ancient Rome _____

_____

82. President who authorized the first military use of nuclear

weapons _____

83. Author of *Silent Spring* who first warned of the effects of

chemical pollution in the 1960s _____

84. American author whose book *The Jungle* prompted

reforms in the meatpacking industry _____

85. Gunfighter who died holding "the dead man's hand" in

Deadwood, Dakota Territory, 1876 _____

86. Infamous Revolutionary War turncoat _____

87. Dancer of the "seven veils" _____

88. American president during construction of the Panama

canal _____

89. English navigator who rediscovered the Sandwich Islands

in 1778 _____

90. Leader of the struggle for the independence of India _____

91. Long-imprisoned South African black nationalist leader

_____

92. "Wonder Boy" actor/director who frightened America with

his radio adaptation of *War of the Worlds* _____

93. English architect who designed St. Paul's Cathedral _____

_____

94. English Queen who reigned during the religious persecution

of Protestants in the sixteenth century _____

_____

95. Cuban revolutionary killed in Bolivia _____

96. Most famous Spanish surrealist painter _____

97. American author of *The Feminine Mystique* _____

98. American seamstress credited with creation of the

first American flag _____

99. English Captain of the HMS *Bounty* _____

Test 9B
WHAT'S THEIR LINE?

WHAT DO (OR DID)
THE FOLLOWING
PEOPLE DO FOR A
LIVING?

100. Billy Sunday _____

101. Clarence Darrow _____

102. Gabriel García Márquez ____ _____

103. Michelangelo Antonioni _____

104. I. M. Pei _____

105. Martha Graham _____

106. Lillian Hellman _____

107. Jane Addams _____

108. Billy Martin _____

109. Helen Gurley Brown _____

110. Margaret Mead _____

111. Frank Buck _____

112. John DeLorean _____

113. Wynton Marsalis _____

114. Harland Sanders _____

115. Cesar Chavez _____

116. H. L. Mencken _____

117. Lynn Stallmaster _____

118. Lester Maddox _____

119. Don King _____

120. Ottorino Respighi _____

121. Bill Monroe _____

122. Annie Leibowitz _____

123. Jackson Pollack _____

124. Red Adair _____

125. John Kenneth Galbraith _____

126. Gorgeous George _____

127. Cordell Hull _____

128. Chuck Yeager _____

129. Joe Montana _____

130. Dick Cheney _____

131. Stephen Hawking _____

132. Sandra Day O'Connor _____

133. Pat Schroeder _____

134. Sally Jessie Raphael _____

135. Ally Sheedy _____

136. Jean-Pierre Rampal _____

137. Leona Helmsley _____

138. Jane Goodall _____

139. Nadine Gordimer _____

140. Swifty Lazar _____

141. King Sunny Ade _____

142. Boris Becker _____

143. Mario Andretti _____

144. Stephen Jay Gould _____

145. William Bennett _____

146. Ivan Boesky _____

147. Bernie Pacheco _____

148. Garry Trudeau _____

149. Marvin Mitchelson _____

150. H. Ross Perot _____

151. Bob Marley _____

152. Muriel Spark _____

153. Grant Tinker _____

154. Tom Hanks _____

155. Lee Iacocca _____

156. Satchel Paige _____

157. Benjamin Spock _____

158. Georgia O'Keeffe _____

159. Gypsy Rose Lee _____

160. Jerome Robbins _____

161. Itzhak Perlman _____

162. Jackie Presser _____

163. Oprah Winfrey _____

164. Jack Kerouac _____

165. Wernher von Braun _____

166. Christie Brinkley _____

167. Woodward and Bernstein _____

168. Masters and Johnson _____

169. Claude Pepper _____

170. Tom Braden and Pat Buchanan _____

171. Ferrante and Teicher _____

172. Willie Shoemaker _____

173. Billie Jean King _____

174. Joan Baez _____

175. Barbara Bush _____

176. Geraldine Ferraro _____

177. Annie Sullivan _____

178. Joan Jett _____

179. Barbara Jordan _____

180. Shirley Chisholm _____

181. Christie Hefner _____

182. Ruth Westheimer _____

183. Winnie Mandela _____

184. Miriam Makeba _____

185. George Will _____

186. Jane Pauley _____

187. Bruce Lee _____

188. Barry Commoner _____

189. Paul Robeson _____

190. Ellen Goodman _____

191. Margaret Bourke-White _____

192. Lily Tomlin _____

193. Mark Rothko _____

194. Alan Paton _____

195. Tammy Faye Bakker _____

196. Isadora Duncan _____

197. David Dinkins _____

198. Busby Berkeley _____

199. Rupert Murdoch _____

200. Francis Gary Powers _____

201. Morton Downey, Jr. _____

202. Manuel Noriega _____

203. Jim Fixx _____

204. Pauline Kael _____

Now we're going to have a little vocabulary quiz. What people do for a living is one point of contact, of connection. The ritual of introduction always has to do with establishing what people do for a living. Sometimes those occupations are opaque and mysterious because we don't know what the words mean, what the titles or classifications indicate. Take this test and see if you know what the following people do.

TEST 9C
WHAT'S THEIR LINE? PART II

BRIEFLY DEFINE THE FOLLOWING:

205. An *ecdysiast* _____

206. A *numismatist* _____

207. A *philatelist* _____

208. A *paleontologist* _____

209. A *proctologist* _____

210. An *arbitrager* _____

211. A *key grip* _____

212. A *cartographer* _____

213. A *cryptographer* _____

214. A *demographer* _____

215. A *urologist* _____

216. A *podiatrist* _____

217. A *hydrogeologist* _____

218. An *underwriter* _____

219. An *ICU nurse* _____

220. A *docent* _____

221. A *dockwalloper* _____

222. A *phlebotomist* _____

223. A *phrenologist* _____

224. A *lepidopterist* _____

225. An *ornithologist* _____

226. An *ichthyologist* _____

227. A *gandy dancer* _____

228. A *best boy* _____

229. A *girl Friday* _____

230. An *ethnomusicologist* _____

231. A *PIO* _____

232. A *DDS* _____

233. A *cosmetologist* _____

234. A *haberdasher* _____

235. A *horticulturist* _____

236. A *herpetologist* _____

237. A *croupier* _____

238. A *roadie* _____

239. An *impresario* _____

240. A *pit boss* _____

241. A *diva* _____

242. An *assayer* _____

243. A *semanticist* _____

244. A *concierge* _____

245. A *soothsayer* _____

246. A *sommelier* _____

247. A *detailer* _____

248. A *water witch* or *dowser* _____

249. A *hod carrier* _____

250. A *graphologist* _____

251. A *granger* _____

252. An *ombudsman* _____

253. A *gerontologist* _____

254. A *gofer* _____

255. An *actuary* _____

256. A *curator* _____

257. A *picador* _____

258. A *taxonomist* _____

259. A *tout* _____

260. A *toxicologist* _____

261. An *epidemiologist* _____

262. A *mangler* _____

263. A *choker setter* _____

264. A *topographer* _____

265. An *agronomist* _____

266. A *stevedore* _____

267. A *timpanist* _____

268. A *lexicographer* _____

269. A *bailiff* _____

270. An *oenologist* _____

271. An *oddsmaker* _____

272. An *acupuncturist* _____

273. A *pedagogue* _____

274. A *pedodontist* _____

275. A *gigolo* _____

276. A *rhinologist* _____

277. A *vivisectionist* _____

278. A *gonif* or *ganef* _____

279. A *gondolier* _____

TEST 9D
HOW SOON WE FORGET:
America's Most Admired

WE'RE FAIRLY QUICK TO AWARD HONORS AND DISTINCTIONS IN THIS COUNTRY, BUT WE'RE EQUALLY QUICK TO FORGET THE CONTRIBUTIONS PEOPLE MAKE. THE DEMANDS OF THE PRESENT AND OF THE FUTURE TURN EVEN RECENTLY FAMOUS PEOPLE INTO THE DIMLY REMEMBERED OR THE ENTIRELY FORGOTTEN.

EACH YEAR FOR THE LAST FORTY YEARS, THE GALLUP POLL HAS COMPILED A LIST OF THE PUBLIC FIGURES MOST ADMIRED BY THE AMERICAN PEOPLE. IS FAME FLEETING? LET'S FIND OUT BY TESTING HOW WELL YOU KNOW OR REMEMBER THESE MOST ADMIRED MEN AND WOMEN OF THE LAST FORTY YEARS.

280. In 1946, Harold Stassen was the ninth most admired man in the country. Who was he? _____

281. In 1948, Kate Smith was the sixth most admired woman in the United States. Why? _____

282. In 1947, George Marshall was the fifth most admired man. Who was he? _____

283. Clare Boothe Luce made the most admired list every year between 1948 and 1965. What did she do to earn this long admiration? _____

284. In 1949, the eighth most admired man was Bernard Baruch. Who was he? _____

285. June Allyson was the sixth most admired woman in 1951. Who was she? Who is she? _____

286. In 1950, Dr. Ralph Bunche was the ninth most admired man. Who was he? _____

_____

287. Oveta Culp Hobby made the most admired list four years running, from 1952 to 1955. Do you know why? _____

_____

288. In 1956, Dag Hammarskjöld was the eighth most admired man in the country. Why? _____

_____

289. Norma Jean Baker shared the list with Oveta Culp Hobby in 1954. She was better known as _____

290. Eleanor Roosevelt was the most admired woman in 1958. Why? _____

291. Helen Hayes was the fourth most admired woman in 1956. Who is she? _____

292. Dr. Thomas Dooley was widely admired in 1959, making the list at number seven. Why was he admired? _____

_____

293. Helen Keller was perenially admired, making the list some sixteen times. Surely you remember her. _____

_____

294. Douglas MacArthur made the list in 1962. He was _____

_____

295. Pauline Frederick was much admired in 1961 and 1962. Why was she admired? _____

296. Hubert Humphrey was the eighth most admired man in 1965. You remember him, don't you? _____

297. Ngo Diem Nhu was the ninth most admired woman of 1963. She was not an American. Can you be more precise

about who and what she was? _____

298. U Thant was the sixth most admired man in 1966. Who

was U? _____

299. Pearl S. Buck was admired by large numbers of Americans in 1964, 1965, 1966, and 1968. Who was she? _____

300. Who is Vaclav Havel? _____

This completes the test of deeds and the doers of deeds. Now you can check your answers to see how you did at knowing what they did.

TEST 9A ANSWERS

1. The development of the process of pasteurization: Louis Pasteur

2. The first heart transplant: Christiaan Barnard

3. The discovery of gravity: Isaac Newton

4. The Louisiana Purchase: Thomas Jefferson

5. Author of *Utopia* who defied Henry VIII: Sir Thomas More

6. The discovery of the New World: Christopher Columbus

7. The Protestant Reformation: Martin Luther

8. The formation of the Church of England: Henry VIII

9. World War II's most decorated U.S. war hero: Audie Murphy

10. The first man on the moon: Neil Armstrong

11. The first American to orbit the earth: John Glenn

12. The intellectual founders of communism: Karl Marx and Friedrich Engels

13. The head of the Third Reich: Adolf Hitler

14. Two major English romantic poets: William Wordsworth, Samuel Coleridge, John Keats, Percy Shelley, Lord Byron, William Blake

15. The playwright who wrote *Cymbeline:* William Shakespeare

16. Two painters who founded Cubism: Georges Braque and Pablo Picasso

17. The two best known nineteenth-century American feminists: Elizabeth Cady Stanton and Susan B. Anthony

18. The first first lady of the United States: Martha Washington

19. The director of *Birth of a Nation:* D. W. Griffith

20. The scientist who postulated that the earth moves around the sun: Nicolaus Copernicus

21. The leader of the Norman Conquest: William the Conqueror

22. Author of *On the Origin of Species:* Charles Darwin

23. The "face that launched a thousand ships": Helen of Troy

24. Inventor of the phonograph: Thomas Edison

25. The theory of relativity: Albert Einstein

26. The author of the Monroe Doctrine: James Monroe

27. The creator of Mickey Mouse: Walt Disney

28. The man credited with devising the assembly line method of industrial production: Henry Ford

29. Inventor of the wireless radio: Guglielmo Marconi

30. Man in charge of the New Deal: Franklin Roosevelt

31. Father of psychoanalysis: Sigmund Freud

32. Assassin of Abraham Lincoln: John Wilkes Booth

33. World's first four-minute-miler: Roger Bannister

34. Ruler of England at the height of its empire: Queen Victoria

35. First solo nonstop transatlantic flight aviator: Charles Lindbergh

36. Best-remembered Greek ruler during the Golden Age: Pericles

37. The Queen of the Nile: Cleopatra

38. Inventor of the printing press: Johannes Gutenberg

39. Author of *Gulliver's Travels:* Jonathan Swift

40. English king during the American Revolution: King George III

41. Ethiopian King during the Italian invasion: Haile Selassie

42. Fascist ruler of Spain during World War II: Francisco Franco

43. Director of "Do the Right Thing": Spike Lee

44. *Rites of Spring* composer: Igor Stravinsky

45. Russian Communist leader killed while in exile in Mexico: Leon Trotsky

46. Spanish explorer who discovered Florida: Juan Ponce de León

47. Leader of American forces at the Battle of New Orleans during the War of 1812: Andrew Jackson

48. American woman known as the "Moses of her people" for helping hundreds of slaves escape to the North on the Underground Railroad: Harriet Tubman

49. Composer most associated with the music known as ragtime: Scott Joplin

50. *Time* magazine's "Man of the Decade" for the 1980s: Mikhail Gorbachev

51. Woman who became known as the "mother of the civil rights movement" when she refused to give up her seat on a bus in the 1950s: Rosa Parks

52. Black leader of the Back to Africa Movement: Marcus Garvey

53. British general who defeated Napoleon at Waterloo: Arthur Wellington

54. Persian poet who wrote *Robaiyat* (The *Rubaiyat*): Omar Khayyám

55. Austrian-Czech author of *The Trial:* Franz Kafka

56. English poet who wrote *The Faerie Queene:* Edmund Spenser

57. American author of *The Scarlet Letter:* Nathaniel Hawthorne

58. Austrian composer of *The Magic Flute:* Wolfgang Amadeus Mozart

59. U.S. composer of "Stars and Stripes Forever": John Philip Sousa

60. French author of *The Second Sex:* Simone de Beauvoir

61. Central figure in the Savings and Loan Scandal, Head of Lincoln Savings: Charles Keating

62. English author of *Leviathan:* Thomas Hobbes

63. American author of *Portnoy's Complaint:* Philip Roth

64. Richard Nixon's opponent in the 1968 presidential race: Hubert Humphrey

65. Convicted of slapping a Beverly Hills cop: Zsa Zsa Gabor

66. Philippine ruler ousted by Corazon Aquino: Ferdinand Marcos

67. Military leader of American forces in Vietnam War: William Westmoreland

68. Russian-born Israeli woman who served as prime minister of Israel, 1969–1974: Golda Meir

69. The Virgin Queen: Elizabeth I

70. The "King of Rock 'n' Roll": Elvis Presley

71. Founding editor of *Ms.* magazine: Gloria Steinem

72. English author of *Middlemarch:* George Eliot

73. U.S. born British poet who penned *The Wasteland:* T. S. Eliot

74. Pathfinder who established the Cumberland Trail: Daniel Boone

75. Soviet leader who said, "We will bury you": Nikita Khrushchev

76. American President who called the Soviet Union "the evil empire": Ronald Reagan

77. Presidential candidate who wanted us to read his lips: George Bush

78. Man who stood in the door of the University of Alabama registration office to block integration: George Wallace

79. Famous British nurse during the Crimean War: Florence Nightingale

80. VP candidate who was "no Jack Kennedy": J. Danforth Quayle

81. Leader of an uprising of gladiators in Ancient Rome: Spartacus

82. President who authorized the first military use of nuclear weapons: Harry Truman

83. Author of *Silent Spring* who first warned of the effects of chemical pollution in the 1960s: Rachel Carson

84. American author whose book *The Jungle* prompted reforms in the meatpacking industry: Upton Sinclair

85. Gunfighter who died holding "the dead man's hand" in Deadwood, Dakota territory, 1876: Wild Bill Hickok

86. Infamous Revolutionary War turncoat: Benedict Arnold

87. Dancer of the "seven veils": Salome

88. American president during construction of the Panama canal: Theodore Roosevelt

89. English navigator who rediscovered the Sandwich Islands in 1778: Captain James Cook

90. Leader of the struggle for the independence of India: Mohandas Gandhi

91. Long imprisoned South African black nationalist leader: Nelson Mandela

92. "Wonder Boy" actor/director who frightened America with his radio adaptation of *War of the Worlds:* Orson Welles

93. English architect who designed St. Paul's Cathedral: Christopher Wren

94. English Queen who reigned during the religious persecution of Protestants in the sixteenth century: Mary I, or "Bloody Mary"

95. Cuban revolutionary killed in Bolivia: Che Guevara

96. Most famous Spanish surrealist painter: Salvadore Dali

97. American author of *The Feminine Mystique:* Betty Friedan

98. American seamstress credited with creation of the first American flag: Betsy Ross

99. English Captain of the HMS *Bounty:* William Bligh

100. Billy Sunday: Evangelist

101. Clarence Darrow: Lawyer

102. Gabriel García Márquez: Author

103. Michelangelo Antonioni: Film director

104. I. M. Pei: Architect

105. Martha Graham: Dancer/choreographer

106. Lillian Hellman: Writer/playwright

107. Jane Addams: Social worker

108. Billy Martin: Baseball player/manager

109. Helen Gurley Brown: Publisher/editor

110. Margaret Mead: Anthropologist

111. Frank Buck: Showman/animal trainer

112. John DeLorean: Automaker

113. Wynton Marsalis: Jazz and classical musician

114. Harland Sanders: Fried chicken magnate

115. Cesar Chavez: Labor/civil rights leader

116. H. L. Mencken: Writer/journalist/gadfly

117. Lynn Stallmaster: Casting director for TV and films

118. Lester Maddox: Governor/segregationist

119. Don King: Fight promoter

120. Ottorino Respighi: Composer

121. Bill Monroe: Bluegrass musician

122. Annie Leibowitz: Celebrity photographer

123. Jackson Pollack: Artist

124. Red Adair: Firefighter

125. John Kenneth Galbraith: Economist/scholar

126. Gorgeous George: Wrestler

127. Cordell Hull: Statesman

128. Chuck Yeager: Aviator

129. Joe Montana: Quarterback

130. Dick Cheney, Secretary of Defense

131. Stephen Hawking: Scientist/cosmologist

132. Sandra Day O'Connor: Supreme Court justice

133. Pat Schroeder: Congresswoman

134. Sally Jessie Raphael: Talk show hostess

135. Ally Sheedy: Actress

136. Jean-Pierre Rampal: Flautist

137. Leona Helmsley: Hotel owner

138. Jane Goodall: Naturalist

139. Nadine Gordimer: Antiapartheid novelist

140. Swifty Lazar: Hollywood agent

141. King Sunny Ade: African musician

142. Boris Becker: Tennis player

143. Mario Andretti: Auto racer

144. Stephen Jay Gould: Paleontologist

145. William Bennett: former Secretary of Education. Current drug policy czar

146. Ivan Boesky: Convicted arbitrager

147. Bernie Pacheco: The fight doctor

148. Garry Trudeau: Cartoonist

149. Marvin Mitchelson: Divorce lawyer

150. H. Ross Perot: Industrialist/tycoon

151. Bob Marley: Reggae star/musician

152. Muriel Spark: Author

153. Grant Tinker: TV producer

154. Tom Hanks: Actor

155. Lee Iacocca: Businessman

156. Satchel Paige: Baseball pitcher

157. Benjamin Spock: Pediatrician/author

158. Georgia O'Keeffe: Artist

159. Gypsy Rose Lee: Ecdysiast

160. Jerome Robbins: Choreographer

161. Itzhak Perlman: Violinist

162. Jackie Presser: Union boss

163. Oprah Winfrey: Talk show hostess/actress

164. Jack Kerouac: Beat Generation writer

165. Wernher von Braun: Rocket scientist

166. Christie Brinkley: Model

167. Woodward and Bernstein: Journalists

168. Masters and Johnson: Sex researchers

169. Claude Pepper: Senator/champion of the elderly

170. Tom Braden and Pat Buchanan: Political commentators

171. Ferrante and Teicher: Pianists

172. Willie Shoemaker: Jockey

173. Billie Jean King: Tennis star

174. Joan Baez: Singer/activist

175. Barbara Bush: First lady

176. Geraldine Ferraro: Politician

177. Annie Sullivan: Teacher

178. Joan Jett: Rock star

179. Barbara Jordan: Congresswoman/civil rights activist

180. Shirley Chisholm: Politician/educator

181. Christie Hefner: Corporation president

182. Ruth Westheimer: Talk show hostess/sex expert

183. Winnie Mandela: Leader of South African black nationalists

184. Miriam Makeba: Singer

185. George Will: Columnist/commentator

186. Jane Pauley: Television personality/news anchor

187. Bruce Lee: Kung fu legend/film star

188. Barry Commoner: Scientist/environmentalist

189. Paul Robeson: Persecuted black actor/singer

190. Ellen Goodman: Columnist/commentator

191. Margaret Bourke-White: Photographer

192. Lily Tomlin: Comedienne/actress

193. Mark Rothko: Painter

194. Alan Paton: Author

195. Tammy Faye Bakker: TV evangelist

196. Isadora Duncan: Dancer

197. David Dinkins: Mayor of New York City

198. Busby Berkeley: Film choreographer

199. Rupert Murdoch: Publisher/wheeler-dealer

200. Francis Gary Powers: Pilot/spy

201. Morton Downey, Jr.: Talk show host

202. Manuel Noriega: Deposed military dictator

203. Jim Fixx: Runner/fitness writer

204. Pauline Kael: Film critic

TEST 9C ANSWERS

205. An ecdysiast is a stripper.

206. A numismatist is a coin collector.

207. A philatelist is a stamp collector.

208. A paleontologist studies fossils.

209. A proctologist treats diseases of the large intestine.

210. An arbitrager is a financial markets manipulator/profiteer.

211. A key grip is a boss handyman on a movie set.

212. A cartographer is a map maker.

213. A cryptographer decodes or writes secret messages.

214. A demographer is a populations statistician.

215. A urologist treats diseases of the urogenital or urinary tract.

216. A podiatrist deals with care of the feet.

217. A hydrogeologist studies rock formations in search of water.

218. An underwriter determines risk for insurance companies.

219. An ICU nurse is an intensive care nurse.

220. A docent is a museum tour guide.

221. A dockwalloper is a longshoreman.

222. A phlebotomist is a therapeutic bloodletter.

223. A phrenologist "reads" bumps on the head.

224. A lepidopterist is a student of butterflies.

225. An ornithologist is a student of birds.

226. An ichthyologist is a fish zoologist.

227. A gandy dancer belongs to a railroad section gang.

228. A best boy is an apprentice grip or gaffer on a movie set.

229. A girl Friday is a loyal helper or assistant.

230. An ethnomusicologist studies the music of particular cultures or regions.

231. A PIO is a public information officer.

232. A DDS is a doctor of dental surgery.

233. A cosmetologist is skilled in the application of cosmetics.

234. A haberdasher is a hat salesman.

235. A horticulturist grows fruits, vegetables, flowers, and other plants.

236. A herpetologist is a reptile/amphibian zoologist.

237. A croupier is in charge of a gambling table/game.

238. A roadie travels with a rock group and helps in travel and setting up for a show.

239. An impresario leads an opera or ballet company.

240. A pit boss supervises games in a portion of a gambling establishment.

241. A diva is a lead female singer in an opera.

242. An assayer analyzes ore, alloy, drugs, and the like to determine their composition.

243. A semanticist studies the origins, meanings, and relationships of words.

244. A concierge is a head porter at a hotel.

245. A soothsayer makes predictions.

246. A sommelier is a wine steward.

247. A detailer is a person who does detail work on cars in order to ready them for sale.

248. A water witch or dowser searches for water or other substances using a forked branch or stick.

249. A hod carrier carries mortar or bricks.

250. A graphologist analyzes handwriting.

251. A granger is a farmer.

252. An ombudsman is a public official who acts to protect the rights of citizens.

253. A gerontologist is a specialist in the field of aging.

254. A gofer runs errands and does other menial tasks.

255. An actuary calculates statistical risks for insurance companies.

256. A curator oversees a museum or similar organization.

257. A picador is a horseman in a bullfight who pricks the neck muscles of the bull to weaken it.

258. A taxonomist is a classifier of objects.

259. A tout sells tips, particularly at horse races.

260. A toxicologist is a poison specialist.

261. An epidemiologist studies epidemics.

262. A mangler presses sheets and other flat pieces of fabric using a mangle iron.

263. A choker setter is a logger who sets the cables to haul logs.

264. A topographer specializes in mapping the surface features of a region.

265. An agronomist is a specialist in farm management.

266. A stevedore works on a waterfront loading and unloading ships.

267. A timpanist is a percussionist who plays the timpani (kettledrums).

268. A lexicographer writes and/or compiles dictionaries.

269. A bailiff is a deputy who maintains order in a courtroom or who delivers orders to appear in court.

270. An oenologist is a wine maker.

271. An oddsmaker calculates the odds or advantages in a betting or competitive situation.

272. An acupuncturist treats disease or pain by the insertion of needles in particular parts of the body.

273. A pedagogue is a teacher.

274. A pedodontist is a children's dentist.

275. A gigolo is a man who is a paid companion to a woman.

276. A rhinologist is a nose doctor.

277. A vivisectionist conducts research experiments on animals.

278. A gonif or ganef is a thief.

279. A gondolier is an Italian boatman.

TEST 9D ANSWERS

280. Harold Stassen: The young mayor of Minneapolis, Minnesota

281. Kate Smith: A fervently patriotic singer

282. George Marshall: World War II hero and drafter of the Marshall Plan for Europe

283. Clare Boothe Luce: Playwright, diplomat, and U.S. representative

284. Bernard Baruch: Industrial and economic advisor to the U.S. government in World Wars I and II

285. June Allyson: Actress

286. Dr. Ralph Bunche: First black man to be a divisional head in the State Department; was awarded the Nobel Peace Prize in 1950

287. Oveta Culp Hobby: First female cabinet member, Secretary of Health, Education and Welfare; and won the Distinguished Service Medal in World War II, first woman to do so

288. Dag Hammarskjöld: Secretary general of the United Nations, 1954–1961

289. Norma Jean Baker: Actress Marilyn Monroe

290. Eleanor Roosevelt: Former first lady and a dedicated humanitarian

291. Helen Hayes: First lady of the American theater

292. Dr. Thomas Dooley: Wrote an anti-Communist book based on his experiences treating thousands of refugees from North Vietnam

293. Helen Keller: Blind and deaf crusader, writer, and lecturer

294. Douglas MacArthur: Five-star general who served in World Wars I and II and was recalled from command in Korea by President Harry Truman

295. Pauline Frederick: First woman news commentator—first with ABC, then with NBC

296. Hubert Humphrey: Liberal senator and vice president under Lyndon Johnson; ran for president against Richard Nixon in 1968 and lost

297. Ngo Diem Nhu: Wife of the president of South Vietnam

298. U Thant: Burmese diplomat; Secretary general of the United Nations, 1962–1972

299. Pearl S. Buck: Author

300. Vaclav Havel: Playwright, poet, and provisional president of Czechoslovakia

SCORING

This is a difficult test, but the people and things listed here are worth knowing about. Of these questions, how many did you know?

251–300: Acutely knowledgeable. You know what people do and have done.

201–250: Keenly well-informed, but some things have escaped your notice. This scoring range is still well above average for this test.

151–200: Not at all bad. There is much you know, probably much more than this score reflects. There were hundreds of other questions you might have been asked that you would have known.

101–150: We're getting into a marginal range here. If you scored in this range, you are sure to encounter much each day—in print, on television, and in conversation—that is bewildering to you.

100 or less: The farther down on this scale you are, the more you know you need to know.

CHAPTER TEN

GOOD TO KNOW

In this chapter we will test a wide range of knowledge, some of it admittedly trivial, some of it perhaps essential. The test items found here are shorter than those in the earlier tests. They are also more varied. The sections are arranged thematically and even those items that might be considered trivial are good to know.

We'll initiate this series of tests by challenging how well you know the words that lurk behind the countless acronyms and initials used as a kind of verbal shorthand in much of our contemporary discourse. Because we live in a society that is always pressed for time, a society that is increasingly bureaucratic, we tend to shorten or abbreviate things whenever we can. We turn government agencies, common phrases, and all sorts of groups and committees into acronyms and initials, a bewildering alphabet soup of letters that stand for words we sometimes forget—or never knew.

TEST 10A
INITIAL IMPRESSIONS

1. Yuppies seek to be awarded MBAs, which stands for _____

_____

2. Yuppies often hope to work for IBM, which stands for _____

_____

3. If they succeed, they expect VIP treatment, meaning treatment for a _____

4. Rising to the top, they become CEOs, which are _____

_____

5. If they get in trouble, they sometimes prompt the scrutiny of the SEC, which is the _____

6. They send out memos under the initials FYI, which stands for _____

7. Yuppies can be imperious, demanding things PDQ, which is _____

8. Some have high IQs, short for _____

9. A yuppie in college might be a BMOC, which stands for

_____

_____

10. Some yuppies work for firms engaged in negotiating LBOs, which are _____

Those should have been fairly easy. Most of the acronyms or initials are likely to be encountered in print or in the workplace nearly any day of the week. If you did well, your appetite should be whetted for greater challenges to your "initial" understanding. Try these.

TEST 10B
MORE INITIAL IMPRESSIONS

11. Country people know that RFD stands for _____

_____

12. Most people know that C.O.D. stands for _____

_____

13. Trade unionists know that the ILGWU is the _____

_____

14. Republicans know that GOP stands for the _____

_____

15. Veterans of World War I know that the AEF was the _____

_____

16. All veterans know that AWOL means _____

_____

17. AIDS is _____

_____

18. Doctors know and join the AMA, which is the _____

_____

19. Recovering alcoholics know that the DTs are _____

_____

20. Many children know that UNICEF is the _____

_____

TEST 10C
INITIAL IMPRESSIONS:
Your Tax Dollars at Work

WHAT DO THE FOLLOWING INITIALS REPRESENT?

21. FDA _____

22. VA _____

23. FHA _____

24. BLM _____

25. AEC _____

26. NASA _____

27. BIA _____

28. DOD _____

29. EPA _____

30. FDIC _____

TEST 10D
A.K.A. (ALSO KNOWN AS)

WHILE SOME GOVERNMENT AGENCIES OBSCURE THEIR IDENTITIES BEHIND INITIALS, SOME PEOPLE INVENT NEW NAMES FOR THEMSELVES OR RECEIVE NAMES INVENTED FOR THEM BY OTHERS.

IN THE FOLLOWING SECTION YOU WILL FIND A LIST OF NAMES OR SOBRIQUETS ASSOCIATED WITH PEOPLE WHO WERE MORE WIDELY KNOWN BY OTHER NAMES. BY WHAT OTHER NAMES HAVE THE FOLLOWING PEOPLE BEEN REMEMBERED?

31. "Old Hickory" _____

32. Archibald Leach _____

33. The "It" Girl _____

34. Gary Hartpence _____

35. William Bonney _____

36. The Butcher of Lyon _____

37. Allen Stewart Konisberg _____

38. Cassius Marcellus Clay _____

39. Robert Zimmerman _____

40. "The Little Tramp" _____

41. Richard Starkey _____

42. The Great Emancipator _____

43. The Jersey Lily _____

44. Charles Lutwidge Dodgson _____

45. "Old Blood and Guts" _____

46. "The Desert Fox" _____

47. Richard Penniman _____

48. The Immortal Bard _____

49. "The Boss" _____

50. The King of Torts _____

TEST 10E
MURDERER'S ROW

WE NOW ENTER DARKER TERRAIN. HISTORY IS NOT ONLY A RECORD OF GLORIOUS ACCOMPLISHMENTS, BUT OF TERRIBLE MISDEEDS. PERHAPS IT IS EVEN MORE IMPORTANT THAT WE REMEMBER THE WRONGDOERS.

IN THE FOLLOWING TEST, SUPPLY THE TIME (CENTURY OR DECADE) AND PLACE IN WHICH THESE PEOPLE CARRIED OUT THEIR NEFARIOUS ACTIVITIES.

51. Charles Starkweather . . . . . Time_____Place_____
52. Kenneth Bianchi . . . . Time_____Place_____
53. Torquemada . . . . Time_____Place_____
54. Caligula . . . . Time_____Place_____
55. Dr. Josef Mengele . . . . Time_____Place_____
56. Lee Harvey Oswald . . . . . . Time_____Place_____
57. Son of Sam . . . . Time_____Place_____
58. Idi Amin . . . . Time_____Place_____
59. Nicolae Ceausescu . . . . Time_____Place_____
60. Genghis Khan . . . . Time_____Place_____
61. Jack the Ripper . . . . Time_____Place_____
62. Reverend Jim Jones . . . . Time_____Place_____
63. Josef Stalin . . . . Time_____Place_____
64. "Dutch" Schultz . . . . Time_____Place_____
65. Sirhan Sirhan . . . . Time_____Place_____
66. William Quantrill . . . . Time_____Place_____
67. James Earl Ray . . . . Time_____Place_____
68. Mark David Chapman . . . . Time_____Place_____
69. Gary Gilmore . . . . Time_____Place_____
70. John Wilkes Booth . . . . Time_____Place_____

TEST 10F
TITLE ROLES

ON A BRIGHTER NOTE, IN THIS NEXT SECTION TRY YOUR MEMORY OF FAMOUS MOTION PICTURES. WHILE THIS KNOWLEDGE MAY NOT BE ESSENTIAL, OR EVEN IMPORTANT, THESE THINGS DO COME UP ALL THE TIME. MOVIE PEOPLE, IT HAS BEEN SAID, ARE THE AMERICAN ARISTOCRACY. IDENTIFY THE ACTRESS OR ACTOR WHO PORTRAYED THE TITLE CHARACTER IN EACH OF THE FOLLOWING MOVIES.

71. *Annie Hall* _____

72. *Citizen Kane* _____

73. *Norma Rae* _____

74. *Jezebel* _____

75. *Captain Blood* _____

76. *Marty* _____

77. *Arthur* _____

78. *Alfie* _____

79. *Rocky* _____

80. *Butch Cassidy and the Sundance Kid* (two answers) _____

_____

81. *The Graduate* _____

82. *Top Gun* _____

83. *Urban Cowboy* _____

84. *The Quiet Man* _____

85. *The Man Who Would Be King* _____

86. *The Hustler* _____

87. *The Godfather* (two answers) _____

88. *The Virginian* (screen version) _____

89. *Funny Girl* _____

90. *Auntie Mame* _____

TEST 10G
CULTURAL LANDMARKS:
The Great Works

RAISING OUR BROWS A BIT, NOW WE WILL DETERMINE IF YOU KNOW WHO WROTE THE GREAT BOOKS OF WESTERN CIVILIZATION. THE FOLLOWING BOOKS, OFTEN MORE REVERED THAN READ, ARE GENERALLY AGREED TO BE AMONG THE FINEST WORKS OF OUR CULTURE. DO YOU KNOW WHO WROTE THEM?

91. *The Iliad* and *The Odyssey* _____

92. *The Republic* _____

93. *The Decameron* _____

94. *Don Quixote* _____

95. *The Divine Comedy* _____

96. *The Prince* _____

97. *Pilgrim's Progress* _____

98. *Robinson Crusoe* _____

99. *Paradise Lost* _____

100. *Candide* _____

101. *Faust* _____

102. *Leaves of Grass* _____

103. *Anna Karenina* _____

104. *Les Misérables* _____

105. *Walden* _____

106. *Crime and Punishment* _____

107. *Huckleberry Finn* _____

108. *Ulysses* and *Finnegan's Wake* _____

109. *Remembrance of Things Past* _____

110. *Pride and Prejudice* _____

TEST 10H
CULTURAL LANDMARKS:
The Visual Arts

IN THIS SECTION, YOU ARE MORE LIKELY TO HAVE SEEN A PRINT OF THE PAINTINGS IN QUESTION THAN TO REMEMBER THE NAME OF THE PAINTER. IN ANY CASE, SEE HOW WELL YOU DO AT MATCHING THE ARTIST WITH HIS MOST FAMOUS WORK.

111. *Starry Night*

112. *Christina's World*

113. *The Persistence of Memory*

114. *Nude Descending a Staircase*

115. *American Gothic*

116. *The Scream*

117. *Nighthawks*

118. *The Bath*

119. *Mona Lisa*

120. *The Garden of Earthly Delights*

121. *Hunters in the Snow*

122. *Bar at the Folies-Bergere*

123. *Demoiselles d'Avignon*

124. *The Birth of Venus*

125. *"Blue Boy"*

126. *Venus of Urbino*

127. *Sunday Afternoon on the Island of La Grand Jatte*

128. *At the Moulin Rouge*

129. *Giovanni Arnolfini and his Bride*

130. *Ceiling of the Sistine Chapel*

a. Hieronymus Bosch

b. Sandro Botticelli

c. Pieter Brueghel

d. Mary Cassatt

e. Salvador Dali

f. Leonardo da Vinci

g. Marcel Duchamp

h. Thomas Gainsborough

i. Edward Hopper

j. Édouard Manet

k. Michelangelo

l. Edvard Munch

m. Pablo Picasso

n. Georges Seurat

o. Titian

p. Henri de Toulouse-Lautrec

q. Jan van Eyck

r. Vincent van Gogh

s. Grant Wood

t. Andrew Wyeth

TEST 101
WHO WROTE THE BOOK OF LOVE? A POP QUIZ

THERE ARE FEW THINGS MORE UBIQUITOUS IN AMERICAN CULTURE THAN POPULAR MUSIC. IT MAY OR MAY NOT BE TRIVIAL, BUT IT SURELY IS GOOD TO KNOW A THING OR TWO ABOUT THE MUSIC THAT SWIRLS AROUND OUR EARS AT ALL TIMES. HOW MUCH DO YOU KNOW ABOUT THIS MUSIC? WE'LL BEGIN WITH A TEST OF SOME OF THE TOP ONE HUNDRED SINGLE HIT RECORDS OF THE PAST TWENTY-FIVE YEARS. WHAT RECORDING ARTISTS ARE ASSOCIATED WITH THE FOLLOWING HIT RECORDS?

131. "(I Can't Get No) Satisfaction" _____

132. "I Wanna Hold Your Hand" _____

133. "I Heard It Through the Grapevine" _____

134. "Respect" _____

135. "The Dock of the Bay" _____

136. "Stop! In the Name of Love" _____

137. "Born to Run" _____

138. "My Generation" _____

139. "Louie, Louie" _____

140. "Dancin' in the Streets" _____

141. "Hotel California" _____

142. "Light My Fire" (name lead singer and group) _____

_____

143. "Hold On, I'm Coming" _____

144. "Little Red Corvette" _____

145. "Bridge Over Troubled Water" _____

146. "Every Breath You Take" _____

147. "Pride (In the Name of Love)" _____

148. "Papa's Got a Brand New Bag" _____

149. "Anarchy in the U.K." _____

150. "Like a Rolling Stone" _____

Test 10J
CLASSICAL KNOWLEDGE

IN *THE MERCHANT OF VENICE*, SHAKESPEARE WROTE, "THE MAN THAT HATH NO MUSIC IN HIMSELF,/NOR IS MOVED WITH CONCORD OF SWEET SOUNDS,/IS FIT FOR TREASONS, STRATAGEMS AND SPOILS." IF YOU LOVE MUSIC EVEN A BIT, YOU SHOULD BE ABLE TO MATCH THE MUSIC MAKER WITH THE MUSIC. WHO WROTE THE FOLLOWING WELL-KNOWN COMPOSITIONS?

151. *Pictures at an Exhibition* _____

152. *The Planets* _____

153. *The Moonlight Sonata* _____

154. *The 1812 Overture* _____

155. *The William Tell Overture* _____

156. *The Brandenburg Concertos* _____

157. *The Four Seasons* _____

158. *Thus Spake Zarathustra* _____

159. *Bolero* _____

160. *Scheherazade* _____

161. *Eine Kleine Nachtmusik* _____

162. *The Trout Quintet* _____

163. *Carmen* _____

164. *Fountains of Rome* _____

165. *La Bohème* _____

166. *Amahl and the Night Visitors* _____

167. *The Bartered Bride* _____

168. *Appalachian Spring* _____

169. *An American in Paris* _____

170. *Pomp and Circumstance* _____

a. Mozart
b. Beethoven
c. Mussorgsky
d. Rimsky-Korsakov
e. Bach
f. Holst
g. Rossini
h. Vivaldi
i. Ravel
j. Wagner
k. Tchaikovsky
l. Respighi
m. Bizet
n. Schubert
o. Copland
p. Puccini
q. Menotti
r. Smetana
s. Elgar
t. Gershwin

IF MUSIC BE THE FOOD OF LOVE, THEN WE HAVE A QUITE NATURAL SEGUE FROM THE LAST SECTION TO THIS ONE OF FAMOUS LOVERS. HISTORY, LITERATURE, MYTH, AND FOLKLORE CELEBRATE GREAT AND UNDYING LOVES. IN THIS SECTION, MATCH THE LOVER TO HER IMMORTAL LOVE.

JOHN NANCE GARNER IS PROBABLY BEST REMEMBERED FOR HAVING SAID THAT THE VICE-PRESIDENCY "WASN'T WORTH A BUCKET OF WARM SPIT." PERHAPS REMEMBERING THEM ISN'T WORTH MUCH MORE, BUT THE POSITION STANDS IN SUCCESSION TO ONE OF THE MOST IMPORTANT POSTS IN THE WORLD. CAN YOU MATCH THE PRESIDENTS (OR PRESIDENTIAL CANDIDATES) WITH THEIR RUNNING MATES?

TEST 10K
MATCHMAKING

171. Francesca _____	a.	Rhett
172. Isolde _____	b.	Abelard
173. Josephine _____	c.	Romeo
174. Desdemona _____	d.	Heathcliff
175. Scarlett _____	e.	Orpheus
176. Heloise _____	f.	Antony
177. Eurydice _____	g.	Othello
178. Catherine _____	h.	Paolo
179. Juliet _____	i.	Napoleon
180. Cleopatra _____	j.	Tristan

TEST 10L
VEEPS

Presidents (Or Candidates)	Running Mates
181. Lincoln _____	a. Colfax
182. Goldwater _____	b. Agnew
183. McGovern _____	c. Ferraro
184. Mondale _____	d. Muskie
185. Dukakis _____	e. Garner
186. F. D. Roosevelt _____	f. Bentsen
187. Eisenhower _____	g. A. Johnson
188. Grant _____	h. Nixon
189. Humphrey _____	i. Miller
190. Nixon _____	j. Eagleton/Shriver

Test 10M
CHILDREN'S LIT

WE'LL CLOSE OFF THIS CHAPTER BY SEEING HOW WELL YOU REMEMBER SOME OF THE DELIGHTS OF CHILDHOOD. FEW BOOKS HAVE THE IMPACT OR ARE MORE FONDLY REMEMBERED THAN THE BOOKS OF CHILDHOOD. BUT DO YOU REMEMBER WHO CREATED THEM?

191. *Treasure Island* _____

192. *Nancy Drew* _____

193. *Peter Pan* _____

194. *Alice in Wonderland* _____

195. *The Little Prince* _____

196. *Little Women* _____

197. *Winnie the Pooh* _____

198. *Black Beauty* _____

199. *Heidi* _____

200. *Pinocchio* _____

That brings to a close a potpourri of questions ranging from identifying what initials stand for in some well-known government agencies to the loved and remembered books of childhood. Little links this knowledge in any thematic way. It's all just "good to know."

TEST 10A ANSWERS	1. MBA stands for Master of Business Administration
	2. IBM stands for International Business Machines
	3. VIP is Very Important Person
	4. CEOs are Chief Executive Officers
	5. SEC is Securities and Exchange Commission
	6. FYI stands for For Your Information
	7. PDQ is Pretty Damn Quick
	8. IQ stands for Intelligence Quotient
	9. BMOC stands for Big Man on Campus
	10. LBOs are Leveraged Buyouts

TEST 10B ANSWERS	11. RFD stands for Rural Free Delivery
	12. C.O.D. stands for Collect on Delivery
	13. ILGWU is the International Ladies Garment Workers Union
	14. GOP stands for the Grand Old Party
	15. AEF was the American Expeditionary Force
	16. AWOL means Absent Without Leave
	17. AIDS is the Acquired Immune Deficiency Syndrome
	18. AMA is the American Medical Association
	19. DTs are Delirium Tremens
	20. UNICEF is the United Nations International Children's Emergency Fund

TEST 10C ANSWERS	21. FDA is the Food and Drug Administration
	22. VA is the Veterans Administration
	23. FHA is the Federal Housing Administration
	24. BLM is the Bureau of Land Management
	25. AEC is the Atomic Energy Commission
	26. NASA is the National Aeronautics and Space Administration

27. BIA is the Bureau of Indian Affairs

28. DOD is the Department of Defense

29. EPA is the Environmental Protection Agency

30. FDIC is the Federal Deposit Insurance Corporation

TEST 10D ANSWERS

31. "Old Hickory" was the nickname of Andrew Jackson

32. Archibald Leach went on to become Cary Grant

33. The "It" Girl was the sobriquet of Clara Bow

34. Gary Hartpence was the given name of Gary Hart

35. William Bonney is better remembered as Billy the Kid

36. The Butcher of Lyon was christened Klaus Barbie

37. Allen Stewart Konisberg became famous as Woody Allen

38. Cassius Marcellus Clay preferred the name Muhammad Ali

39. Robert Zimmerman changed his name to Bob Dylan

40. "The Little Tramp" was created by Charlie Chaplin

41. Richard Starkey is better known as Ringo Starr

42. The Great Emancipator was, of course, Abraham Lincoln

43. The Jersey Lily was the name that gilded Lillie Langtry

44. Charles Lutwidge Dodgson is better remembered as Lewis Carroll

45. "Old Blood and Guts" was General George Patton

46. "The Desert Fox" was the name given to German General Erwin Rommel

47. Richard Penniman is known to the world as Little Richard

48. The Immortal Bard is William Shakespeare

49. "The Boss" is what his fans call Bruce Springsteen

50. The King of Torts was a nickname given flamboyant lawyer Melvin Belli

TEST 10E ANSWERS

51. Charles Starkweather—murderer and fugitive in the midwestern United States in the late 1950s

52. Kenneth Bianchi, "The Hillside Strangler"—serial killer, United States, West Coast, 1970s

53. Torquemada—grand inquisitor of the Spanish Inquisition in the fifteenth century

54. Caligula—Roman emperor noted for cruelty, first century A.D.

55. Dr. Josef Mengele—chief physician at Auschwitz death camp in Poland, 1943–1944

56. Lee Harvey Oswald—accused assassin of President John F. Kennedy in Dallas, Texas, 1963

57. Son of Sam, or David Berkowitz—deranged serial murderer in New York City, 1970s

58. Idi Amin—Ugandan dictator responsible for the torture and murder of thousands of opposition supporters in the 1970s

59. Nicolae Ceausescu—Romanian dictator. Executed during revolution in December, 1989

60. Genghis Khan—Mongol conqueror in twelfth and thirteenth centuries, noted for his cruelty

61. Jack the Ripper—unidentified perpetrator of a series of gruesome murders in London in 1888

62. Reverend Jim Jones—cult leader who oversaw the mass suicide of more than nine hundred followers in Guyana in 1978

63. Josef Stalin—Soviet leader whose policies led to the deaths and deportations of millions of innocent people

64. "Dutch" Schultz, or Arthur Flegenheimer—leader of a New York and New Jersey crime syndicate in the 1920s and 1930s

65. Sirhan Sirhan—assassin of Robert F. Kennedy in Los Angeles, California, 1963

66. William Quantrill—ruthless guerrilla leader in Kansas and Missouri in 1860s

67. James Earl Ray—assassin of Martin Luther King, Jr., in Memphis, Tennessee, 1968

68. Mark David Chapman—murderer of John Lennon in New York in 1980

69. Gary Gilmore—murderer of two students of Brigham Young University in 1976, subject of a book by Norman Mailer

70. John Wilkes Booth—assassin of President Abraham Lincoln in Washington, D.C., in 1865

TEST 10F ANSWERS

71. Annie Hall was played by Diane Keaton

72. Citizen Kane was played by Orson Welles

73. Norma Rae was played by Sally Field

74. Jezebel was played by Bette Davis

75. Captain Blood was played by Errol Flynn

76. Marty was played by Ernest Borgnine

77. Arthur was played by Dudley Moore

78. Alfie was played by Michael Caine

79. Rocky was played and played and played by Sylvester Stallone

80. Butch Cassidy and the Sundance Kid were played by Paul Newman and Robert Redford

81. The Graduate was played by Dustin Hoffman

82. Top Gun was played by Tom Cruise

83. The Urban Cowboy was played by John Travolta

84. The Quiet Man was played by John Wayne

85. The Man Who Would Be King was played by Sean Connery

86. The Hustler was played by Paul Newman

87. The Godfather was played by Marlon Brando and Robert De Niro

88. The Virginian (screen version) was played by Gary Cooper

89. Funny Girl was played by Barbra Streisand

90. Auntie Mame was played by Rosalind Russell

TEST 10G ANSWERS	91. *The Iliad* and *The Odyssey* were written by Homer
	92. *The Republic* was the work of Plato
	93. *The Decameron* was written by Boccaccio
	94. *Don Quixote* was written by Cervantes
	95. *The Divine Comedy* was written by Dante
	96. *The Prince* was written by Machiavelli
	97. *Pilgrim's Progress* was written by John Bunyan
	98. *Robinson Crusoe* was written by Daniel Defoe
	99. *Paradise Lost* was written by John Milton
	100. *Candide* was the work of Voltaire
	101. *Faust* was written by Goethe
	102. *Leaves of Grass* was written by Walt Whitman
	103. *Anna Karenina* was written by Tolstoy
	104. *Les Misérables* was written by Victor Hugo
	105. *Walden* was written by Thoreau
	106. *Crime and Punishment* was written by Dostoyevski
	107. *Huckleberry Finn* was written by Mark Twain
	108. *Ulysses* and *Finnegan's Wake* were written by James Joyce
	109. *Remembrance of Things Past* was written by Marcel Proust
	110. *Pride and Prejudice* was written by Jane Austen
TEST 10H ANSWERS	111. *Starry Night:* **r.** Vincent van Gogh
	112. *Christina's World:* **t.** Andrew Wyeth
	113. *The Persistence of Memory:* **e.** Salvador Dali
	114. *Nude Descending a Staircase:* **g.** Marcel Duchamp
	115. *American Gothic:* **s.** Grant Wood
	116. *The Scream:* **l.** Edvard Munch
	117. *Nighthawks:* **i.** Edward Hopper
	118. *The Bath:* **d.** Mary Cassatt

119. *Mona Lisa:* **f.** Leonardo da Vinci

120. *The Garden of Earthly Delights:* **a.** Hieronymus Bosch

121. *Hunters in the Snow:* **c.** Pieter Brueghel

122. *Bar at the Folies-Bergere:* **j.** Édouard Manet

123. *Demoiselles d'Avignon:* **m.** Pablo Picasso

124. *The Birth of Venus:* **b.** Sandro Botticelli

125. *"Blue Boy":* **h.** Thomas Gainsborough

126. *Venus of Urbino:* **o.** Titian

127. *Sunday Afternoon on the Island of La Grand Jatte:* **n.** Georges Seurat

128. *At the Moulin Rouge:* **p.** Henri de Toulouse-Lautrec

129. *Giovanni Arnolfini and his Bride:* **q.** Jan van Eyck

130. Ceiling of the Sistine Chapel: **k.** Michelangelo

TEST 10I ANSWERS

131. "(I Can't Get No) Satisfaction": The Rolling Stones

132. "I Wanna Hold Your Hand": The Beatles

133. "I Heard It Through the Grapevine": Marvin Gaye

134. "Respect": Aretha Franklin

135. "The Dock of the Bay": Otis Redding

136. "Stop! In the Name of Love": The Supremes

137. "Born to Run": Bruce Springsteen

138. "My Generation": The Who

139. "Louie, Louie": The Kingsmen

140. "Dancin' in the Streets": Martha and the Vandellas

141. "Hotel California": The Eagles

142. "Light My Fire": Jim Morrison of The Doors

143. "Hold On, I'm Coming": Sam and Dave

144. "Little Red Corvette": Prince

145. "Bridge Over Troubled Waters": Simon and Garfunkel

146. "Every Breath You Take": Sting, as solo

147. "Pride (In the Name of Love)": U2

148. "Papa's Got a Brand New Bag": James Brown

149. "Anarchy in the U.K.": Sex Pistols

150. "Like a Rolling Stone": Bob Dylan

TEST 10J ANSWERS

151. *Pictures at an Exhibition:* **c.** Mussorgsky

152. *The Planets:* **f.** Holst

153. *The Moonlight Sonata:* **b.** Beethoven

154. *The 1812 Overture:* **k.** Tchaikovsky

155. *The William Tell Overture:* **g.** Rossini

156. *The Brandenburg Concerto:* **e.** Bach

157. *The Four Seasons:* **h.** Vivaldi

158. *Thus Spake Zarathustra:* **j.** Wagner

159. *Bolero:* **i.** Ravel

160. *Scheherazade:* **d.** Rimsky-Korsakov

161. *Eine Kleine Nachtmusik:* **a.** Mozart

162. *The Trout Quintet:* **n.** Schubert

163. *Carmen:* **m.** Bizet

164. *Fountains of Rome:* **l.** Respighi

165. *La Bohème:* **p.** Puccini

166. *Amahl and the Night Visitors:* **q.** Menotti

167. *The Bartered Bride:* **r.** Smetana

168. *Appalachian Spring:* **o.** Copland

169. *An American in Paris:* **t.** Gershwin

170. *Pomp and Circumstance:* **s.** Elgar

TEST 10K ANSWERS

171. Francesca: **h.** Paolo

172. Isolde: **j.** Tristan

173. Josephine: **i.** Napoleon

174. Desdemona: **g.** Othello

175. Scarlett: **a.** Rhett

176. Heloise: **b.** Abelard

177. Eurydice: **e.** Orpheus

178. Catherine: **d.** Heathcliff

179. Juliet: **c.** Romeo

180. Cleopatra: **f.** Antony

TEST 10L ANSWERS

181. Lincoln: **g.** A. Johnson

182. Goldwater: **i.** Miller

183. McGovern: **j.** Eagleton/Shriver

184. Mondale: **c.** Ferraro

185. Dukakis: **f.** Bentsen

186. F. D. Roosevelt: **e.** Garner

187. Eisenhower: **h.** Nixon

188. Grant: **a.** Colfax

189. Humphrey: **d.** Muskie

190. Nixon: **b.** Agnew

TEST 10M ANSWERS

191. *Treasure Island* was the work of Robert Louis Stevenson

192. *Nancy Drew* was the work of Carolyn Keene

193. *Peter Pan* was the creation of J. M. Barrie

194. *Alice in Wonderland* was created by Lewis Carroll

195. *The Little Prince* was the work of Antoine de Saint-Exupéry

196. *Little Women* was written by Louisa May Alcott

197. *Winnie the Pooh* was brought into the world by A. A. Milne

198. *Black Beauty* was the creation of Anna Sewall

199. *Heidi* was written by Johanna Spyri

200. *Pinocchio* was written by Carlo Collodi

SCORING

Because these two hundred questions range so widely, the scoring is a bit less severe than in earlier tests.

131–200: An excellent score anywhere in this range. You bring much to what you read.

101–130: Still very good. There is much you know about things that are good to know.

61–100: This is getting into a weaker range, meaning that you are hearing and reading many things that puzzle you.

60 or less: Begin reading immediately. There's no time to waste.

CHAPTER ELEVEN

FINDING THE COMMON GROUND

It would take only one generation of forgetfulness to put us back several thousand years.

Dean Tollefson

Whether we like it or not, much of what education demands of us is the ability to organize information. Information alone is of little value unless we can understand how each bit of information relates to the others. It is in this way that we move from rote learning toward coherence, toward a system of relative value and importance, and toward seeing the entire picture and not just a few compelling details.

It is precisely this coherence that the schools are so poor in presenting. We move from classroom to classroom, idea to idea, period to period without anyone providing us with the linkages that allow us to see how economics and politics and literature and history and a hundred other disciplines all relate to one another. Also, quite commonly, we are denied a chronology that would allow us to connect cause with effect, beginnings with outcomes. When my students were tested about when certain major events occurred, their guesses were wildly inaccurate. What is significant about that is not that they would fail a history test, but that they have been denied a sense of the progression, the sequence, that created them and the world they live in. Without such an understanding, they are doomed to live in a world without sense or reason, where things are the way they are because of random chance, a world where human intervention is futile and insignificant because things "just happen." I think that is the message we have inadvertently given a couple of generations of American students, and I think it explains their profound apathy and general disconnectedness.

This chapter, in only the most superficial way, tests your ability to organize what you know and to identify or define relationships between bits of knowledge. It is the smallest step toward order and coherence, a brief nod in the direction of shaping the details into a pattern, either chronological or geographic.

The test you are about to take contains three hundred questions. Each contains three or more bits of information, which means there are over a thousand things to know in the test. In order to do well, you must think your way through it, putting things you know together with things you don't know in order to arrive at reasoned attempts at the correct answers. One thing the test result is bound to indicate is that you know a great deal more than you thought you did. And, whether you do well or poorly on this test, it is not a bad idea first of all to consider those things that have adhered to you, all the things you *do* know.

As I was putting this test together, it became a game with friends, nearly all of whom wanted to supply test questions. From this I learned something fairly fundamental: Constructing tests is perhaps a better way of learning things than taking tests. So, as one of the prescriptive measures for those readers who wish to expand their store of common knowledge, I suggest that you don't stop after taking this last test, but that you begin drafting tests of your own. Can you come up with fifty questions like the ones in this chapter? A hundred questions? In doing so, you'll find that the item you begin a question with will force you to look into encyclopedias, dictionaries, and other reference books for companion items. In doing so myself, I found the exercise to be wonderfully enriching. Looking up one thing, I always turned up something unexpected, something I hadn't known before. If the idea of expanding your knowledge base interests you (and I assume it does, since you have this book in your hand), then I can think of no better way to do it than to draft tests. It doesn't feel like study at all.

All too often, it seems, the purpose of testing in schools is to catch you out when it should be catching you up. Once the school tests have revealed what you don't know, you dutifully turn to the next lesson, the next chapter, the next course. That seems radically foolish on the face of it, but it's standard operating procedure in all the schools I know about, and few students or teachers ever think to question it.

Like the other tests in this book, this one should be used as a springboard to further learning. In this test that should be easy because what you know can combine so readily with what you don't know. This is a difficult test, but it bears clues and spurs to thinking in every question. Have at it . . . and good luck.

TEST 11
COMMONALITIES

IN THE FOLLOWING
SEQUENCES, WHAT
DO THE LISTED
ENTRIES SHARE?
WHAT ENTERPRISE,
OCCUPATION,
CLASSIFICATION, OR
POINT OF
IDENTIFICATION DO
THEY HAVE IN
COMMON?

1. The Schmoos, Sparkle Plenty, Calvin and Hobbes _____

_____

2. shekel, guilder, peseta, lira, cruzeiro, zloty _____

3. Left Bank, Île de la Cite, Montmartre, Montparnasse _____

_____

4. noun, verb, adjective, adverb, article, preposition _____

_____

5. Billy Martin, Casey Stengel, Leo Durocher, Tommy Lasorda

_____

6. tetracycline, penicillin, streptomycin _____

7. op. cit., loc. cit., ibid. _____

8. Neocene, Pliocene, Miocene _____

9. Keats, Shelley, Coleridge, Wordsworth, Byron, Blake _____

_____

10. Arquebus, Pepper Pot, Blunderbuss, Duck's Foot _____

11. Sydney Harbor, Golden Gate, Verrazano-Narrows _____

12. Richmond, Queens, Brooklyn, Bronx, Manhattan _____

_____

13. Gurkha, Bowie, Barlow, Green River, jack _____

14. Mammalia, Amphibia, Reptilia, Insecta, Arachnida _____

_____

15. Mamba, Krait, Coral, Bushmaster _____

16. Andromeda, Orion, Perseus, Cassiopeia, Ursa Major _____

_____

17. Fugard, Hansberry, Albee, Shepard, Mamet _____

_____

18. Ayrshire, Brown Swiss, Guernsey, Holstein-Friesian _____

_____

19. The Father, the Son, and the Holy Ghost _____

20. Superior, Erie, Michigan, Huron, Ontario _____

21. merganser, canvasback, teal, muscovy, wood _____

22. metaphor, simile, allegory, irony, hyperbole _____

23. iambic, trochaic, anapestic, dactylic _____

_____

24. Baby Dodds, Gene Krupa, Buddy Rich, Art Blakey _____

_____

25. oeufs à la neige, crêpes suzette, charlotte russe _____

_____

26. Sancho Panza, Tonto, Paul Drake, Dr. Watson, Robin _____

_____

27. Balzac, Hugo, Verne, de Maupassant, Stendahl, Flaubert

_____

28. Turgenev, Gorky, Dostoyevsky, Gogol, Tolstoy _____

_____

29. Jalisco, Morelos, Yucatán, Chihuahua, Durango, Chiapas

_____

30. Goethe, Mann, Schiller, von Herder, Heine _____

31. Dominguin, Arruza, Manolete, Vasquez, Ortega _____

_____

32. Knopf, Scribner, Godine, Dutton _____

33. Limoges, Haviland, Delft, Belleek _____

34. Marengo, Austerlitz, Arcole, Leipzig, Waterloo _____

_____

35. Gielgud, Guinness, Olivier, Richardson _____

_____

36. Mindanao, Luzon, Cebu, Samar, Mindoro, Panay, Negros

_____

37. Soldier's, Bosworth, Strawberry, Potter's _____

38. thalamus, cerebrum, cerebellum, medulla oblongata _____

39. Stanley Kowalski, Don Vito Corleone, Zapata, Julius Caesar _____

40. Constantin Brancusi, Auguste Rodin, Henry Moore _____

_____

41. trichinosis, schistosomiasis, filariasis, visceral larva migrans _____

42. Hormuz, Magellan, Bosporus, Dardanelles, Gibraltar _____

_____

43. legislative, judicial, executive _____

44. Gettysburg Address, Emancipation Proclamation, Second Inaugural Address _____

45. mansard, gambrel, hipped, gabled _____

46. Nisei, New York, NASDAQ, Pacific, American _____

47. Didion, Beattie, Erdrich, Tyler, Morrison _____

_____

48. Scylla and Charybdis, rock and hard place, devil and the deep blue sea, Hobson's choice _____

_____

49. Hammurabi, Wenceslas, Tut, Farouk _____

50. Ophelia, Polonius, Yorick, Rosencrantz and Guildenstern

51. mutually assured destruction, balance of terror, deterrence

_____

_____

52. Winesap, Jonathan, McIntosh, Crab _____

53. Thomas Caxton, Gutenberg, Ben Franklin _____

54. Mary Wollstonecraft, Elizabeth Cady Stanton, Betty

Friedan _____

55. Viotti, Salieri, Bellini _____

56. Jeff Smith, Paul Prudhomme, Alice Waters, Craig

Claiborne _____

57. Thompson, Beretta, Gatling, Boffers _____

58. Pauline Kael, John Simon, James Agee, Rex Reed _____

59. Jim Bowie, Davy Crockett, William Travis _____

60. Pizzaro, Cortez, Balboa, de León _____

61. Eugene V. Debs, Upton Sinclair, George Bernard Shaw,

Olaf Palme, the Fabians _____

62. Montana, Namath, Tarkenton, Tittle _____

63. Sleepy John Estes, Memphis Slim, Sonny Boy Williamson

_____

64. Feiffer, Trudeau, Schultz, Larson, Ketchum _____

65. Bing Crosby, Rudy Vallee, Mel Torme _____

66. Grimm, Andersen, Barrie, Potter, Carroll _____

67. Mad Anthony Wayne, Tom Paine, Casimir Pulaski _____

_____

68. Locke, Mill, Berkeley, Hume _____

69. Anderson, Te Kanawa, Maria Callas, Pons _____

70. Gladstone, Churchill, Thatcher, Disraeli _____

71. Jimmy Page, Les Paul, Eric Clapton, Chet Atkins _____

_____

72. Josh White, Pete Seeger, Woody Guthrie, Odetta _____

73. Jimmy Rodgers, Bob Wills, Hank Williams, Roy Acuff

_____

74. Mencken, Royko, Breslin, Lippman _____

75. Pyle, Crane, Bierce, Fallaci, Capa, Duncan _____

_____

76. Arbus, Lange, Avedon, Stieglitz, Man Ray _____

77. Ming, T'ang, Han, Shang, Sung _____

78. Estevez, Sheen, Sheedy, Ringwald, Lowe _____

_____

79. Muir, Thoreau, Abbey, Lopez, Commoner _____

_____

80. Wren, Wright, Pei, Le Corbusier _____

81. Stan Getz, Paul Desmond, Johnny Griffin, Zoot Simms

_____

82. Blaze Starr, Tempest Storm, Gypsy Rose Lee _____

83. Artie Shaw, Kay Kaiser, Guy Lombardo _____

84. Bob Denver, Alan Hale, Jr., Tina Louise _____

_____

85. Keith Richards, Brian Jones, Bill Wyman _____

86. Paderewski, Iturbe, Horowitz _____

87. Douglass, Garvey, Du Bois, X _____

88. Christy Mathewson, Bob Feller, Sandy Koufax, Lefty

Gomez _____

89. Will Rogers, Josh Billings, Art Buchwald, Mort Sahl _____

_____

90. Stand Watie, Jim Thorpe, Seatlh, Iron Eyes Cody _____

91. Isadora Duncan, Alvin Ailey, Twyla Tharp _____

92. *Lusitania, Maine, Andrea Doria* _____

93. Theda Bara, Jean Harlow, Jane Russell _____

94. Ephesians, Philippians, Thessalonians, Titus _____

95. Sartre, Camus, de Beauvoir _____

96. Bertolucci, Fellini, Antonioni _____

97. Sligo, Mayo, Clare, Cavan, Tipperary, Killkenny _____

_____

98. declarative, interrogative, exclamatory, imperative _____

_____

99. Fassbinder, Herzog, Reifenstahl, Schell _____

100. *a, e, i, o, u*, and sometimes *y* _____

101. B. B., Billie Jean, Martin Luther, Jr. _____

102. Corso, Ginsberg, Ferlinghetti _____

103. Keaton, Arbuckle, Lloyd, Turpin _____

104. Somoza, Batista, Pinochet, Stroessner _____

105. Whitehead, Archimedes, Godel, Hypatia _____

106. Jackie Robinson, Satchel Paige, Willie Mays _____

107. grouper, flounder, gar _____

108. 1776, 1789, 1917 _____

109. Goebbels, Göring, Himmler, Hess _____

110. Ionic, Corinthian, Doric _____

111. *Cossi fan tutte, The Magic Flute, Parsifal, Rigoletto* _____

_____

112. King, Kissinger, Mother Teresa, Elie Wiesel _____

113. DeBakey, Barnard, Koop _____

114. Lichtenstein, Warhol, Johns _____

115. Stockhausen, Cage, Webern, Schönberg _____

116. Sam Rayburn, Thomas O'Neill, Jim Wright, Tom Foley

_____

117. cumbia, merengue, pachanga _____

118. hansom, landau, phaeton, cabriolet _____

119. nimbostratus, altocumulus, cumulonimbus _____

_____

120. Brown Bess, Long Tom, Big Bertha _____

121. "raining cats and dogs," "cold as hell," "hard as nails"

_____

122. Bauhaus, Georgian, Rococo, Gothic _____

123. succubus, incubus, dybbuk _____

124. Peter the Great, Boris Godunov, Ivan IV _____

125. Mercury, Apollo, Challenger _____

126. Gene Autry, Roy Rogers, Tex Ritter _____

127. phonograph, incandescent electric light, mimeograph

_____

128. Marne, Somme, Gallipoli, Belleau Wood _____

129. Chisholm, Goodnight, Santa Fe _____

130. largo, adagio, andante _____

131. Keeshond, Basenji, Borzoi, Vizsla _____

132. atlatl, catapult, sling _____

133. SDS, Weathermen, Black Panthers _____

134. Masada, Wounded Knee, My Lai _____

135. igneous, sedimentary, volcanic _____

136. Baltimore and Ohio, Trans-Siberian, Tokyo-Osaka _____

137. Albany, Bismarck, Springfield, Sacramento, Olympia
_____

138. crab, lobster, barnacle, crayfish _____

139. femur, tibia, coccyx _____

140. amoeba, spirocyte, paramecium _____

141. Na, Cl, Zr, K, F, Ni _____

142. Tokugawa Shogunate, Meiiji Restoration, Fujiwara _____
_____

143. latke, blintz, tortilla, crepe _____

144. Goodman, Schwerner, Cheney _____

145. Micmac, Maidu, Menominee, Mohawk _____

146. Iago, Fagin, Injun Jim, Dr. Moriarity _____

147. Joe Palooka, the Hit Man, Gentleman Jim Corbett, Jake
LaMotta _____

148. four-in hand, Windsor, sheepshank, half-hitch _____

149. Shinto, Tao, Sufi _____

150. Todd, Warner, Burton, Hilton, Fisher _____

_____

151. St. Thomas, St. Croix, St. John _____

152. Tyler, Taylor, Harrison, Polk, Fillmore _____

_____

153. Clotho, Lachesis, Atropos _____

154. Athos, Porthos, Aramis _____

155. *Pudd'nhead Wilson, A Tramp Abroad, The Gilded Age*

_____

156. Kabuki, Noh, commedia dell'arte _____

157. Bordeaux, Brittany, Cote d'Azur _____

158. Aramaic, Indic, Gaelic, Slavic, Dardic _____

159. Calliope, Euterpe, Erato, Polyhymnia, Clio, Melpomene

Thalia Terpsichore, Urania _____

160. Port de bras, Pas de deux, Arabesque _____

161. ectomorph, endomorph, mesomorph _____

162. Innocent, Gregory, Pius, John Paul _____

163. isosceles, scalene, right, equilateral _____

164. Augustus, Hadrian, Tacitus, Caligula _____

165. Luther, Zwingli, Calvin, Knox, Henry VIII _____

_____

166. Beelzebub, Mephistopheles, Asmodeus _____

167. Philo Vance, Lord Peter Wimsey, Sam Spade, Dick Tracy

_____

168. Dionysus, Aphrodite, Apollo, Eros _____

169. poinard, bodkin, dirk, stiletto _____

170. Conquest, Famine, Pestilence, Death _____

171. Percival, Galahad, Lancelot _____

172. Osiris, Horus, Isis, Set _____

173. Freedom from Want, Freedom from Fear, Freedom of

Worship, and Freedom of Speech and Expression _____

_____

174. waddy, vaquero, drover, gaucho _____

175. Pylades and Orestes, Damon and Pythias, Castor and

Pollux _____

176. Mars, Vulcan, Diana, Bacchus _____

177. bireme, dhow, barkantine, argosy, carrack _____

178. card stacking, ad hominem, testimonial, bandwagon

_____

179. lothario, swain, inamorato _____

180. id, ego, superego _____

181. Agincourt, Hastings, Salamanca, Antietam _____

182. Colossus of Rhodes, Hanging Gardens of Babylon, Temple of Diana at Ephesus, Egyptian Pyramids _____

_____

183. Wellesley, Vassar, Radcliffe, Bryn Mawr _____

184. *Le Monde, Pravda, Die Welt, The Guardian* _____

185. riboflavin, thiamine, pyridoxine, ascorbic acid _____

186. krummhorn, clavier, sackbut, flageolet _____

_____

187. Richard Wright, Langston Hughes, Ralph Ellison _____

_____

188. Vanderbilt, Morgan, Rockefeller _____

189. *Nina, Pinta, Santa Maria* _____

190. Yahoos, Houyhnhnms, Lilliputians _____

191. Anne Boleyn, Jane Seymour, Anne of Cleves, Catherine Howard, Catherine Parr _____

192. Dead Kennedys, Sex Pistols, The Clash _____

193. *Dr. Strangelove, Barry Lyndon, Paths of Glory, 2001* _____

194. tarantella, mazurka, gavotte, hornpipe _____

195. *A Doll's House, Hedda Gabler, An Enemy of the People*

_____

196. *1812 Overture, Swan Lake, The Nutcracker* _____

_____

197. Allenby, Montgomery, Gordon, Kitchener _____

198. Mucha, Rackham, Gorey, Max _____

199. moniker, handle, patronym, appellation _____

200. Zulu, Sepoy, Crimea, Boer, Sudan, Lucknow _____

_____

201. dipsomaniac, tosspot, Bacchante, souse _____

202. Cassatt, O'Keeffe, Moses _____

203. Valentino, Bushman, Fairbanks _____

204. Toni Morrison, Alice Walker, Maya Angelou _____

_____

205. Cripple Creek, Deadwood, Yukon, Sutter's Mill _____

_____

206. Sharps, Spencer, Hawken, Winchester _____

207. Baudelaire, Rimbaud, Mallarmé, Verlaine _____

208. Seurat, Degas, Monet, Pissaro, Renoir, Sisley _____

_____

209. Credit Mobilier, Tweed Ring, Teapot Dome, Watergate

_____

210. Adler, Jung, Horney, Klein, Rogers _____

211. be-bop, hot, cool, fusion, third-stream _____

212. Tarawa, Leyte Gulf, Midway _____

213. Treblinka, Buchenwald, Majdanek, Dachau _____

_____

214. Larry, Moe, Curly, Shemp _____

215. *Fibber McGee and Molly, The Shadow, The Fat Man,*

Allen's Alley, Gangbusters, Inner Sanctum _____

216. bodhrán, tambour, kettle _____

217. Knesset, Bundestag, Diet _____

218. alpaca, llama, guanaco _____

219. *Hard Times, Bleak House, Our Mutual Friend* _____

_____

220. Darrow, Bailey, Mitchelson, Belli _____

221. Sein Fein, Molly MacGuires, IRA _____

222. Wakan-Tanka, Yaweh, Allah, Ormazd, Ahura Mazda ____

_____

223. Plantagenet, Lancaster, Tudor, Stuart, Windsor _____

_____

224. Chelsea, Soho, Piccadily, West End _____

225. Epistemology, Ethics, Aesthetics, Metaphysics, Logic

_____

226. PASCAL, COBOL, ALGOL, APL, ADA _____

227. apse, transept, nave, sacristy _____

228. lancet, ogee, cinquefoil, horseshoe, semicircular _____

_____

229. acute, obtuse, reflex, straight, right _____

230. calabash, calumet, hookah, bong _____

231. stamen, calyx, sepal, petal, pedicel, pistil _____

_____

232. Cerberus, Checkers, Fala _____

233. Adam Smith, David Ricardo, J. M. Keynes, Milton

Friedman _____

234. Orozco, Rivera, Siqueiros _____

235. IWW, Solidarity, UMW, CIO _____

236. anvil, hammer, cochlea, stirrup _____

237. duodenum, cecum, ileum _____

238. emu, kiwi, ostrich, cassowary _____

239. Borges, Garcia Márquez, Fuentes, Vargas Llosa _____

_____

240. Leghorn, Plymouth Rock, Cornish, Rhode Island Red

_____

241. yurt, wickiup, dacha _____

242. Gallica, Catalonia, Castile, Andalusia _____

243. morning star, mace, pike _____

244. impetigo, ecthyma, pyogenic granuloma, cellulitis _____

_____

245. Horace Mann, John Dewey, Clark Kerr, William Bennett

_____

246. Halston, Givenchy, Balenciaga, Lauren, Vionnet _____

_____

247. Stephen Foster, Hoagy Carmichael, Cole Porter _____

248. Hedda Hopper, Liz Smith, Louella Parsons, Rona Barrett

_____

249. Zeppo, Gummo, Harpo _____

250. De Gaulle, Pompidou, Mitterand _____

251. Ottoman, Byzantine, Roman, British _____

252. Azoic, Precambrian, Paleozoic, Mesozoic, Cenozoic _____

_____

253. Ramapithecus, Australopithecus, Homo Erectus

Neanderthal _____

254. borsolino, porkpie, panama, fedora _____ _____

255. psaltery, domra, charango, kithara _____

256. Brahma, Vishnu, Shiva _____

257. Koran, Upanishads, Mishna _____

258. tumeric, cardamon, chervil _____

259. Gabby Hayes, Smiley Burnett, Andy Devine _____

_____

260. Emily, Charlotte, Anne _____

261. Bantu, Ashanti, Xhosa _____

262. right, blue, beluga, narwhal _____

263. Sandra Day O'Connor, Thurgood Marshall, William

Rehnquist _____

264. National Recovery Act, Social Security Act, WPA _____

_____

265. Buddy Holly, The Big Bopper, Richie Valens _____

_____

266. Sea of Tranquility, Sea of Fertility, Sea of Nectar _____

_____

267. *Timon of Athens, Titus Andronicus, Troilus and*

Cressida _____

268. "The Raven," "The Gold Bug," "The Murders in the Rue

Morgue" _____

269. Queeg-Queeg, Ishmael, Ahab _____

270. Cotton Mather, Roger Williams, Increase Mather _____

_____

271. *Limelight, Modern Times, The Gold Rush, City Lights*

_____

272. Mario Cuomo, Huey Long, Jerry Brown, George Wallace

_____

273. Huey, Dewey, Louie _____

274. Larry, Darrell, Darrell _____

275. Dennis Day, Mary Livingstone, Don Wilson, Rochester

_____

276. Red Barber, Ronald Reagan, Mel Allen, Howard Cosell

_____

277. Tinkers, Evers, Chance _____

278. Nancy Lopez, Sam Snead, Lee Trevino, Babe Zaharias

_____

279. Alecto, Tisiphone, Megaera _____

280. Bear Bryant, Knute Rockne, Woody Hayes, Joe Paterno

_____

281. pai gow, faro, monte, chemin de fer _____

282. Preakness, Kentucky Derby, Belmont Stakes _____

283. Johnny Longden, Eddie Arcaro, Willie Shoemaker _____ __

284. Haldeman, Erlichman, Dean, Liddy _____

285. North, Poindexter, Secord, McFarlane _____

286. Wallace, Safer, Reasoner, Bradley, Rooney _____

287. Belushi, Radner, Aykroyd, Chase, Curtin, Newman _____

288. Jelly Roll Morton, Bix Beiderbecke, Kid Ory, King Oliver

289. Freddy Prinze, Lenny Bruce, "Bobcat" Goldthwait _____

290. Johnny Weissmuller, Lex Barker, Elmo Lincoln _____

291. Sing Sing, Attica, Leavenworth, Alcatraz _____

292. Brezhnev, Andropov, Chernenko _____

293. Amundsen, Peary, Cook, Scott _____

294. Gavrilo Princip, John Wilkes Booth, Leon Czolgosz _____

295. Alice, Trixie, Ed, Ralph _____

296. *The Sun Also Rises, A Farewell to Arms, The Old Man and the Sea* _____

297. Elizabeth Gurley Flynn, "Big Bill" Haywood, Joe Hill _____

_____

298. Joseph Smith, Brigham Young, George Watt _____

299. mistral, sirocco, boro, fon, Santa Ana, "the Hawk" _____

300. Valencia, Satsuma, Navel, Osage, King _____

Before checking your answers, you might do well to jot down all the ideas that came to you for test questions of your own, if you haven't been doing that along the way. As you surely noticed, this test is uncommonly eclectic, ranging as it does from classical knowledge to pop culture. Since what we read, hear, and see draw upon all these sources and traditions, it's good to know it all, even though spirited arguments can be made about relative importance. Are you a better person for knowing what you know while remaining steadfastly ignorant of what someone else knows? The answer is most assuredly no. Yet it is common for people to protect themselves from the charge of ignorance in just that way.

     Now it's time to check your answers. Did you find the common ground in common knowledge?

TEST 11 ANSWERS

1. Comic strip characters

2. Monetary units

3. Districts of Paris

4. Parts of speech

5. Baseball managers/coaches

6. Antibiotics

7. Reference citations

8. Geologic epochs, subdivisions of a geologic period

9. English romantic poets

10. Guns

11. Bridges

12. Boroughs of New York City

13. Knives

14. Classes in biologic taxonomy

15. Poisonous snakes

16. Constellations

17. Twentieth-century playwrights/dramatists

18. Breeds of dairy cattle

19. The Christian Holy Trinity

20. The Great Lakes

21. Kinds of ducks

22. Figurative language

23. Meters in prose or poetry; ways of scanning pattern, stress, and rhythm in language

24. Jazz drummers/percussionists

25. Desserts, specifically, French desserts

26. Fictional sidekicks

27. French writers, nineteenth century

28. Russian writers, nineteenth century

29. Mexican states

30. German writers

31. Bullfighters/matadors

32. Publishers

33. China, or places where fine china is produced

34. Napoleonic battles

35. Major actors of twentieth-century British theatre

36. Philippine islands

37. Famous fields

38. Parts of the brain

39. Roles played by Marlon Brando

40. Sculptors

41. Diseases caused by worms

42. Straits

43. The three branches of the U.S. government

44. Speeches/proclamations by Abraham Lincoln

45. Styles of roofs

46. Stock exchanges

47. Contemporary American female writers

48. All expressions for (or allusions to) situations where the choices one has are unpleasantly limited or bad

49. Kings

50. Characters in Shakespeare's *Hamlet*

51. Cold war terms to describe the arm's race and to justify arms buildups in the Soviet Union and the United States

52. Apples

53. Printers

54. Crusaders for women's rights

55. Italian composers

56. Cookbook authors

57. Men who invented specific firearms that took their names

58. Film critics

59. Three who died at the Alamo

60. Explorers

61. Socialists

62. Professional football quarterbacks

63. Blues singers

64. Cartoonists

65. Singers, specifically crooners

66. Authors of classic works for children

67. Heroes of the American Revolution

68. Philosophers of the United Kingdom

69. Opera divas

70. British prime ministers

71. Master guitarists

72. Folk singers

73. Pioneers of country and western music

74. Journalists/columnists

75. Writers/journalists/war correspondents

76. Photographers

77. Chinese dynasties

78. Young actors/actresses collectively dubbed "The Brat Pack"

79. Naturalists/nature writers/ecologists

80. Architects

81. Jazz tenor saxophone players

82. Ecdysiasts/strippers

83. Big band leaders

84. Members of the cast of *Gilligan's Island*

85. Rolling Stones

86. Classical pianists

87. American black leaders

88. Baseball pitchers

89. Humorists/satirists

90. American Indians

91. Dancers/choreographers

92. Famous sunken ships

93. Movie sex symbols

94. Books of the Bible

95. French existentialists

96. Italian film directors

97. Counties in Ireland

98. Types of sentences

99. German film directors

100. Vowels

101. Kings

102. Beat generation poets

103. Silent film comics

104. Latin American dictators

105. Mathematicians

106. Black baseball pioneers

107. Fish

108. Years revolutions took place—specifically, the American, the French, and the Russian

109. Nazis

110. Architectural names for kinds of columns

111. Famous operas

112. Winners of the Nobel Peace Prize

113. Surgeons

114. Pop artists

115. Avant-garde composers

116. Speakers of the House

117. Latin American dances

118. Horse-drawn carriages

119. Types of cloud formations

120. Guns

121. Clichés

122. Architectural styles/periods

123. Demons/supernatural beings

124. Russian rulers

125. Spacecraft

126. Singing cowboys, films, 1930s and 1940s

127. Inventions of Thomas Alva Edison

128. Battles of World War I

129. Famous trails of the American West

130. Musical notations indicating the tempo of the music

131. Breeds of dog

132. Means of launching projectiles/weapons

133. Radical groups of the 1960s

134. Massacres

135. Kinds of rock

136. Well-known railways

137. State capitals

138. Crustaceans

139. Bones

140. Single-celled organisms

141. Symbols of chemical elements

142. Rulers/periods in Japanese history

143. Various kinds of "pancakes"

144. Three civil rights workers killed in Mississippi

145. American Indian tribes

146. Fictional villains

147. Boxers/prize fighters

148. Knots

149. Eastern religions

150. Husbands of Elizabeth Taylor

151. Virgin Islands

152. American presidents/streets of San Francisco

153. The Fates, from Greek mythology

154. The Three Musketeers, from the Dumas book of the same name

155. Books by Mark Twain

156. Traditional Japanese and Italian theater/drama

157. Regions of France

158. Major language groups

159. The Muses, from Greek mythology

160. Terms for balletic moves

161. Body shapes/types

162. Popes of the Catholic Church

163. Kinds of triangles

164. Roman emperors

165. Leaders of the Protestant Reformation

166. Names for Satan, the devil

167. Fictional detectives/sleuths

168. Greek gods

169. Knives

170. The Four Horsemen of the Apocalypse

171. Knights of the Round Table/heroes of Arthurian legend

172. Egyptian gods

173. The Four Freedoms, as set forth by Franklin D. Roosevelt

174. Names by which cowboys are known

175. Famous friendships

176. Roman gods

177. Names for various kinds of boats

178. Propaganda techniques

179. Names for lovers

180. Freudian terms for subdivisions of the psyche

181. Famous battles

182. Four of the Seven Wonders of the Ancient World

183. Ivy League Women's Colleges

184. Newspapers

185. Vitamins

186. Musical instruments from the Renaissance or earlier

187. Twentieth-century black writers

188. Industrialists/robber barons

189. The ships in the fleet of Christopher Columbus

190. Fictional groups from Swift's *Gulliver's Travels*

191. Wives of King Henry VIII

192. Punk rock groups

193. Films directed by Stanley Kubrick

194. Dances

195. Plays by Henrik Ibsen

196. Compositions by Pyotr Ilich Tchaikovsky, Russian composer

197. Famous British generals

198. Artists/illustrators

199. Names for names

200. "Little" wars of the Victorian period, British Empire

201. Names for drunks

202. American female artists

203. Male sex symbols of the silent screen

204. Contemporary American black women writers

205. Gold strikes, mining camps of American/Canadian west

206. Names of rifles

207. Nineteenth-century French poets

208. French Impressionist painters

209. American scandals/abuses of power

210. Freud's disciples/Psychoanalytic pioneers

211. Forms of jazz, jazz variations

212. World War II battles against the Japanese in the Pacific

213. Nazi concentration/death camps

214. The Three Stooges

215. Radio shows from the 1930s and 1940s

216. Drums/percussion instruments

217. Parliaments or governing bodies

218. South American wooly mammals

219. Novels by Charles Dickens

220. Famous lawyers/attorneys

221. Irish resistance groups/movements

222. Names for God, the Supreme Being

223. Royal families/houses of England

224. Sections or districts of London

225. Subdivisions in the study or discipline of philosophy

226. Computer programming languages

227. Parts of a cathedral

228. Kinds (or shapes) of arches

229. Names for various angles

230. Kinds of pipes

231. Parts of a flower

232. Famous dogs

233. Economists/major figures in economics

234. Painters of the Mexican Renaissance in the 1930s

235. Labor unions

236. Parts of the inner ear

237. Parts of the intestine/digestive tract

238. Flightless birds

239. Twentieth-century South American novelists

240. Breeds of chickens

241. Habitations/dwellings

242. Regions in Spain

243. Medieval weaponry/weapons

244. Diseases of the skin, bacterial

245. Educators/educational reformers

246. Fashion designers/couturiers/couturieres

247. American songwriters

248. Gossip columnists

249. Some of the Marx brothers

250. French leaders/presidents

251. Empires

252. Geologic eras (geologic time is measured in eras, periods, and epochs)

253. Stages in human evolution

254. Kinds of hats

255. Stringed musical instruments

256. The Hindu Trinity

257. Holy books—Islam, Hindu, and Jewish, respectively

258. Spices/herbs

259. Sidekicks of the western movies

260. Brontë sisters, English novelists

261. African tribal groups

262. Species of whales

263. Supreme Court justices

264. New Deal programs

265. Three rock stars who died together in a plane crash

266. Areas from the geography of the moon

267. Lesser known Shakespearean plays

268. Works by Edgar Allan Poe

269. Characters from Melville's *Moby-Dick*

270. American Puritan leaders/divines

271. Charlie Chaplin films

272. Governors

273. Comic book characters/Donald Duck's nephews

274. Characters on *Newhart*

275. Characters from the old Jack Benny radio/television show

276. Sports announcers

277. Legendary baseball players famous for stunning double plays

278. Golfing greats

279. The Furies, from Greek mythology

280. College football coaches

281. Games of chance

282. Horse racing's Triple Crown

283. Jockeys

284. Key figures in the Watergate scandal

285. Key figures in the Iran/Contra hearings

286. *60 Minutes* reporters

287. Alumni from *Saturday Night Live*'s early days

288. Jazz pioneers, New Orleans

289. Stand-up comics/comedians

290. Men who played Tarzan in the movies

291. Famous U.S. prisons

292. Russian political leaders/general secretaries preceding Gorbachev

293. Polar explorers

294. Assassins, of Archduke Ferdinand, Abraham Lincoln, and William McKinley, respectively

295. Characters on "The Honeymooners," *The Jackie Gleason Show*

296. Novels by Ernest Hemingway

297. Labor leaders/pioneers of the labor movement in the United States

298. Leaders of the Mormon church

299. Kinds of winds

300. Varieties of oranges

SCORING

Are you a good weaver? Did you do well at weaving together common threads of what you know with what you didn't know? Or did you simply know it all? Here's a rough and arbitrary scale of measurement to allow you to determine how well you did, how much you knew.

251–300: Excellent. You have wide-ranging knowledge and the ability to use that knowledge to draw connections. For you, thinking and knowing come together. You are able to hold your own in any company, so long as you don't get too cocky about it.

201–250: A very good score, which indicates that you know much and can build on what you know to learn more.

151–200: Good. Though not the highest score, it still proves you know a great deal. And just think of all the questions unasked that you could have aced.

101–150: It's starting to get a bit marginal here, but don't despair; you can build on your base of knowledge by researching and making tests of your own, and by reading widely.

100 or less: Chances are, if you're in this category, you gave up on the test in frustration and haven't kept score. There are nearly a hundred questions that most people would consider easy, so you should be interested in knowing more.

Fortunately, this is not so difficult or daunting as it might seem.

PRESCRIPTION FOR FURTHER LEARNING

I once had a teacher who said, "If you want to be a good writer, you need to know the names of things." The same can be said of being a good reader. The more you know, the more pleasure reading brings; and the more you read, the more you know. Education, as currently conducted, does precious little to instill a love of reading. Only about 2 percent of the American people buy books, any books. Most problems in education would be self-correcting if we only provided students with an interest in reading, or if we didn't kill that interest. But dull textbooks and dreary discussions/lectures turn the excitement of reading into pedantic mush.

Do you want to know more? You can do it through reading and thinking about what you've read. Develop the habit of browsing through reference books, where one thing will inevitably lead to another. Construct tests of your own, because in constructing those tests you will organize what you know and will discover areas where your knowledge is not so assured. Finally, it is good to remember that knowing things is not a final destination, it is a point along the way. Even those who know everything in this book, and a great deal more, would be poorer if they count their quest for knowledge complete.

CHAPTER TWELVE
WILLING OURSELVES IGNORANT

By now, if you've been patient and diligent, you've assessed what you know against thousands of bits of information. You've determined how and to what degree you can distinguish between the real and the imagined, between men and women, between various places on the planet. You have found, whatever your scores, that there was much you knew. You've also found, perhaps, that there was much you didn't know. Depending on your disposition and attitudes about knowing, you may have dismissed some questions when you didn't know the answers ("Who cares about that stuff, anyway?"), or you may have felt sheepish and made excuses for yourself ("I used to know that, but I forgot it"). Perhaps the tests have reminded you of how various the world is, and have rekindled some areas of curiosity. Quite frankly, many of the questions were constructed to stimulate curiosity.

Learning really begins when we confront and confess our ignorance, when we choose to open the doors to knowledge. You, the reader of this book, have by that reading already identified yourself as one who thinks knowledge is important. In taking the tests, you confronted and confessed what you didn't know.

Constructing these tests was a bit like taking them; some were fun to do, others were a strain. In the time it took me to do them, the world took on a new cast and became more interesting. Everything became a potential test question. Every time something came up—in conversation, in reading, on the news—I began to wonder whether others knew about that thing. Where once I had assumed everyone knew roughly the same things, I began to listen with a keen ear for what people might not know. I began trying out test questions on friends and relatives. This, however, can be a most dangerous activity and I advise you to use this book with care. If you get in the habit of bombarding people with test questions, you may find yourself with more knowledge, but with fewer friends.

Tests have personalities. Some are inviting, diverting, engaging, and fun, and others are stern, commanding, recriminating, and judgmental. If you look at this book as one large test, then its personality is decidedly schizophrenic. Some sections are playful and teasing, others are portentous and imperious. In some places, the questions rejoice in the bounty of interesting things to know; in other places, the questions despair about all that we need to know that escapes us. It is useful, perhaps, since our lives are plagued and embroidered by so many tests—on the job, at the Department of Motor Vehicles, at school, or at the entrance to school—that we keep in mind there are people behind these test questions, that someone is structuring an order of value, a prioritization, a hierarchy of importance. The more we know about things, the more power we have as individuals to accept or reject that order of importance, that personal judgment, that committee of experts who constructed the test and determined value. Common knowledge doesn't make us common. Since we all interpret what we know in different ways, knowing things is a way of becoming more distinct, more ourselves. Knowing things doesn't make us uniform; it enhances our diversity.

There is no fault to be found in not knowing, unless your ignorance is accompanied by indifference. The argument implicit in this book is that it is "good to know," but increasingly I am aware that such an apparently innocuous and self-evident idea is not shared by everyone. Students, who by definition would seem to be seekers of knowledge, often reject knowing virtually anything and everything they deem irrelevant to their majors and their career aspirations. I remember a student evaluation of a colleague of mine, a history teacher. The student wrote, "I don't like his history class; he dwells on the past too much." I remember seeing a student selling back his American literature text. A friend called out to him, "Whatcha doin'? Sellin' your book?" The student replied, "Yep, ain't nothin' I need in here," and then drop-kicked the book in the direction of his friend; the whispered voices of the American experience went sailing through the air. I remember the professor who told of her astonishment when, some six weeks into a course on women in literature, she gave a little test and found that in spite of her daily use of the term *feminism*, most students in the class had little or no idea what it meant. Two students thought feminism meant being afraid of mice. I think of the Spanish teacher who had tears in her eyes when she found out that not one of her third-semester college Spanish students had heard of Cervantes. And I think also of the student who wrote that "a Siberian shot an Australian hare, thus setting off World War I."

There seems simply to be no widely shared knowledge, nothing we can draw upon to make analogies or allusions. Look for the book or poem that has been read by all students in any college classroom. Such a book, let alone body of books, is not to be found.

Add to that the mass of misinformation and wrongheadedness found in any of those same college classrooms, let alone in the public at large, and the whole business of communication gets significantly more difficult. Comedians confine their material to what they call "lifestyle" humor because they know that a joke about current events or a satirical jibe containing some historical reference will strike the audience dumb. "I can't spend five minutes explaining perestroika in order to make a joke about it," one comic laments.

Try any of the tests in this book on any college student or class. The misinformation and the misunderstandings will both amuse and dismay. "Dannell Boom" died at the Alamo, along with Louis and Clark. The first man in space was Louis Armstrong. Jimmy Carter was the first man to authorize the military use of the atomic bomb. Ragtime was a musical form invented by Bach. The dancer who danced the dance of the seven veils was "Burishnakov." Woodrow Wilson devised the Monroe Doctrine. King Arthur was the leader of England during the American Revolutionary War. And, when asked to list any American writer or novelist, the majority of students in my American literature survey class named Shakespeare.

Think of those inept joke-tellers who always leave out a crucial part of the joke so that when they get to the punch line the joke makes no sense. Think of a movie with blotches on the sound track so that only intermittent bits of dialogue are heard. Think of a novel with every other page missing. Then think of your education and wonder if it wasn't a bit like that joker, that movie, that novel. Unless you were uncommonly fortunate, your education came at you in very much those ways. And, unless your sense of wonder and curiosity somehow escaped the schools intact, it is likely that the joke remains unfunny, the movie incoherent, the novel a perplexity.

It is not the ultimate answers education should provide, of course. We are all left to solve those mysteries for ourselves.

Still, education could help us on our separate quests if it told a coherent tale. It could, I think, make the loneliness of being human less lonely. It could provide us with linkages, a sense of kinship with the past. It could, if done well, reduce intolerance, not through a more effective accretion of facts and data, but through an integration of those facts, that data. It could do all that, and more, if what we were taught were brought to life with more vivifying detail; if the early years of our schooling were not so riddled with falsehood, tedium, and distortion.

Less than half of the eligible voters in the United States bother to cast ballots. About 25 percent of the American people go to college, yet fewer than 2 percent make up the market for books, any books. To me that suggests a quarter of the population seeks higher education, and the majority of those people leave college having been robbed of any further curiosity. Is it too much to expect that an education, even one that ends at the high school level, give us an understanding of our national past (that past is only about four hundred years of history, after all), and an awareness of where in the world we are? Should we not expect that some twelve years of classroom time might allow us to know how geography prefigures politics and, to some degree, destiny? Would it not be possible to expect that we could graduate from high school (or even college) familiar with the major writers and thinkers of our culture? Could we not reasonably expect that by graduation we would have read at least one major novel? Currently, we can expect none of these things.

It's been said that a good teacher is an ignorant person learning. One thing I've learned is just how valuable and how fragile a culture is. It cannot be perpetuated by confining it to scholars (as was done during what was once called the Dark Ages when monks and monasteries were the repositories of knowledge), nor can it be vital and sustaining if it is only stored in computer memory banks. Libraries, unused, may sit idle while madness governs the streets. So it has come to me, after many years of doing the chore, just how necessary and how central the task of education is, and how each generation must commit to it all over again, dragging our baggage into speech because in that baggage, as burdensome as it may be, are things we need. Without such baggage we forget who we are, lose track of our intended destinations, are, to use the metaphor, unclothed. Teaching has taught me what many have learned before: that civilization is a thin and fragile thing, that insanity and chaos are always lurking at the edges, that caring about the past, about other cultures, about the world we live in is only another way of loving ourselves. Losing that love, we grow more violent, value everything less, forget what is noble in us, and can therefore see nobility in no one else.

So it is "good to know," I declaim. But what is good to know? My answer is generic: It's all good to know. It all comes at us, and we should be open to it, not to accept it as all of equal value, but so that we can make our individual judgments about its relative importance. Fads and fashions change; a writer considered great in one era is devalued in another; reputations of painters, statesmen, and ideas fluctuate downward and upward from time to time. But, like the rain forests, it all must be kept alive because we never know what will be useful, either to each of us as individuals, or to the culture as a whole.

Schools should be expected to give us enough "common" knowledge for us to build on, enough commonly shared cultural information so that we can talk with one another easily. We should know, in broad outline, the history of the world, the history of our country. We should know our major writers and what they told us about how we have been shaped by being alive on this continent, with this history. We should expect them to teach us and our children the continuity we inhabit. We should be entitled to know how the systems work: political, solar, social, ecological, and economic. We should be able to expect, as we cannot expect now, that exposure to the educational system will not serve to kill an interest in further education. We should expect, above all, that schools should instill a love of reading just as a menu can make one hungry. Schools should turn out people who can enter a bookstore and not be bewildered. We should expect, demand even, that our children have read enough so that they can recognize charlatans when confronted with them, discern nonsense when it is thrust upon them, know right behavior as only literature and philosophy can teach us right behavior. In order for all of this to happen, we must expect that schools will have students read *real* books, not processed pap. The administrators of such schools will have to be selected not on the basis of their ambition, but on the basis of their dedication; the teachers of such schools will have to be spurred by a cultural assurance that their society values what they do. Teaching must cease to be the thing that people do who cannot think of anything else to do. The narrowing of academic disciplines, requiring that people become narrow and specialized, should be called into question.

And we should individually commit to the value of knowing. Schools cannot perpetuate values unless those values are reflected in the society they serve. There are two kinds of damage done by ignorance: one is to the individual, the other is to the culture. As individuals, we are stung by our ignorance each time it is exposed. The accumulation of these feelings can do much to undermine self-confidence and self-worth. Over time, we shrink from things that might challenge us, avoid people whose knowledge makes us uncomfortable. We let our ignorance define us, limit our choices. When ignorance rules us, we cease to grow.

This book contains some of the things you are left with—this cultural heritage, this data base. It is everywhere. It is a part of you, of us. Should you forget it, or disdain it, you will not be who you are, we will not be who we are.

No loss, perhaps. But they are here, after all, these effects, ideas, trinkets, weapons, events, documents. They are notes to us, these things. We are joined to the people who left them behind. Good people, bad people, troubled people, enlightened people. They left us messages in bottles that floated up on shores of time. We ignore them at our peril. And this ignorance is not bliss, because we are doomed to learn everything—everything—over and over.

We confirm our significance when we accept knowledge, when we know that it is good to know. We honor being human with this simple idea. The doors to knowing are everywhere; we need only open ourselves and they will open.